TABLE OF CONTENTS

Top 20 Test Taking Tips

1. Carefully follow all the test registration procedures
2. Know the test directions, duration, topics, question types, how many questions
3. Setup a flexible study schedule at least 3-4 weeks before test day
4. Study during the time of day you are most alert, relaxed, and stress free
5. Maximize your learning style; visual learner use visual study aids, auditory learner use auditory study aids
6. Focus on your weakest knowledge base
7. Find a study partner to review with and help clarify questions
8. Practice, practice, practice
9. Get a good night's sleep; don't try to cram the night before the test
10. Eat a well balanced meal
11. Know the exact physical location of the testing site; drive the route to the site prior to test day
12. Bring a set of ear plugs; the testing center could be noisy
13. Wear comfortable, loose fitting, layered clothing to the testing center; prepare for it to be either cold or hot during the test
14. Bring at least 2 current forms of ID to the testing center
15. Arrive to the test early; be prepared to wait and be patient
16. Eliminate the obviously wrong answer choices, then guess the first remaining choice
17. Pace yourself; don't rush, but keep working and move on if you get stuck
18. Maintain a positive attitude even if the test is going poorly
19. Keep your first answer unless you are positive it is wrong
20. Check your work, don't make a careless mistake

Human Development

Theories and models

Psychoanalytic theory of gender identification

Freud purposed the psychoanalytic theory of gender development. This theory, while largely disputed today, held a lot of weight for many years after it was introduced. Freud theorized in the oedipal complex that young boys unconsciously fall in love with their mother and wish to marry her. This unconscious wish forces the child to act, "just like daddy" so that he might win his mother's love. The corresponding theory for female gender identification was first proposed by Freud and called the Electra complex by Carl Jung. This theory is more complicated than that of the oedipal complex. Freud postulated that when a girl realizes she doesn't have a penis blames her mother believing she has been castrated. She then attempts to win over the love of the father that she may become pregnant and substitute a pregnancy for a penis.

Social learning theory

Another theory of gender identification is the social learning theory. Behind this theory is the idea that children learn to be a boy or a girl in the same way they learn other social behaviors. For example, a brother and sister dress in their mother's high heeled shoes, the mother scolds the son but admires the daughter thus the children learn that boys do not wear high heeled shoes but girls do. The cognitive development theory states that children place themselves in the role of male or female and then place importance on doing "boy" or "girl" things. Lastly is the idea that the brain is set up with an area marked gender and under that the subsections male and female. This is known as the gender schema theory. Unfortunately this theory does not hold up to intense scrutiny as there are many people who see themselves as a little bit of both.

Jean Piaget's theories on cognitive development

Piaget wrote that there are four stages of cognitive development in children. Sensory-motor is the first stage and lasts from birth to age 2. It is in this stage that a child learns that an object exists even when she can't see it; this is known as object permanence.

From ages 2 to 7 children are in the preoperational stage. Piaget believed that children in this stage are egocentric, incapable of seeing the world from outside of their own point of view, and that they do not understand conservation, the concept that objects may have an equal amount even if they are of different sizes. Piaget termed his next stage, from the age of 7 to 11, the concrete operations stage. It is at this time that children begin to see that things like numbers are solid (concrete). The final phase in this theory is the formal operations stage. Abstract reasoning begins to form around the age of 12 and people continue to develop this skill into adulthood.

Personality theories of Erich Fromm

Fromm described two different types of personal freedom in his model of personality development. In order to become a mentally healthy individual a person must first have all of his basic needs met. Basic needs include food, shelter and clothing. Having these needs met is the first order of freedom. The second order of freedom, which will increase his personal potential, relies on finding a meaningful job and love based on mutual respect. Without this second type of freedom he will survive but not thrive. Fromm listed capitalism and religion as two major barriers to reaching the second stage of personal freedom. He believed that mental problems occur when a person hasn't found his freedom. He encouraged everyone to play throughout life and to find joy in simple things.

Socio-cultural theory of cognitive development

The socio-cultural theory of cognitive development proposed by Lev Vygotsky is in direct contrast to the theories of Piaget. Vygotsky believed that children learn by interacting with other people. Children build their knowledge bit by bit from playing with other children and engaging in activities with adults. Reaching levels of cognitive development has less to do with the age of the child and far more to do with the child's level of social skills. Children who have good social skills learn far more quickly than those with poor social skills. Vygotsky's main area of research was language development in children. Recent research has found more support for the socio-cultural model and less for Piaget's cognitive development theory.

Ecological systems theory

The ecological systems theory of development defines four systems that Urie Bronfenbrenner felt were necessary to study in able to completely understand an individual's personality. First, is the micro system which looks at the places in which a person has direct interaction with the environment. These places might include the individual's house of worship, workplace or home. The mesosystem includes situations that affect each other through the individual such as stress at home spilling over to the workplace. Next, is the exosystem which are things that the person does not experience themselves but which have some effect their life, for example the person's boss have a bad day at home and bringing the stress to the workplace. Last, is the macrosystem which are beliefs and laws which are part of the overall environment and affect the other inner systems.

Social identity theory

Henri Tajfel's theory of social identity equates the development of personality with the desire to obtain and keep a positive self-concept. Self-concept is made up of personal and social identity. Personal identity is defined as those things which make a person unique. Social identity refers to the groups one identifies with and uses to describe oneself, Muslim, liberal, or white collar worker for example. Any group a person identifies with is though of as the "in-group" with the opposite being the "out-group".

Three strategies that bolster the self-image in regards to social identity are "exit", "pass', and "voice". Exit refers to leaving a group which is no longer seen as positive to the self image. Likewise, pass is the behavior of not joining, passing up, a group because a person doesn't feel the group is good enough for them. Finally, voice refers to the entire group's response to an outside threat or slander.

Cognitive behavior therapy

There are many different therapies which fall under the umbrella of cognitive behavior therapy. However, all of the therapies have three things in common, they are inwardly focused, the importance is placed on the client's reaction to the environment, and behavioral change must begin with cognitive change.

Rational-emotive and rational behavior therapy both insist on the patient monitoring their thoughts so that they can realize when situations are likely to trigger maladaptive thinking. Self-instruction therapy allows a child to learn to be her own teacher by observing and modeling appropriate behaviors. Systematic rational restructuring instructs clients to respond to the situation directly rather than to their perception of the situation. Stress inoculation works by teaching patients to use adaptive behaviors at very low levels of stress and gradually building up to very stressful situations. Problem solving therapy instructs the client to understand the problem, make a goal, brainstorm solutions, rate the possible solutions, and implement the chosen solution. A cognitive behavioral approach for depression is self-control therapy which helps the patient regain control of their own thoughts and behaviors.

Crisis theory

Rudolph Moos listed three categories that help explain how people cope in a crisis situation. Illness-related factors make up the first category. These factors include the severity of the illness and how the illness will be treated. The second category deals with the patient's personality and background. Two examples are age and self esteem. Environmental factors, both social and physical make up the third category. Moos also listed behaviors which would continue to help a patient cope better. Behaviors that deal with coping to the illness directly are learning to live with the symptoms, adjusting to the hospital environment and forming good relationships with medical caregivers. Furthermore he defined four behaviors crucial for positive psychosocial functioning: controlling negative emotions; keeping up self-esteem; keeping up friendships; and making preparations for what may happen later.

Problem-solving theory

Some people are not natural problems solvers or through mental illness have lost the ability to solve problems easily. Problem-solving therapy works to re-teach the client to solve problems effectively. There are four stages to problem solving. First, information about the problem is gathered. Possible solutions are thought up in the second stage. The third stage is when solutions are implemented. The final stage is the evaluations stage at which time the person reflects on the successfulness of the problem solving exercise. J.P. Greenlo stated that there are three types of problems. Arrangement problems demand that objects be arranged in such a way that solutions are formed. The second category of problems proposed by Greenlo demand a pattern be formed in order to reach the solution. Transformation is the last category of problems. These problems give the question and the answer but require the solver to find the steps that led from one to the other.

Psychodynamic theory

The psychodynamic theory of human development was first explained by Sigmund Freud. Freud believed that there were three parts to an individual's personality. The first part to develop is the id which is made up of a person's most primal desires. The id wants only pleasure and does not concern itself with how pleasure is obtained. The next function of personality to arise is the ego. The ego attempts to fulfill the desires of the id. The final stage of development is the superego which arises from the ego and is a person's moral voice. The id is mainly driven by the libido or psychosexual energy. The libido is focused on different parts of the body during the course of human development. From birth until the age of one the libido obtains gratification orally through sucking or chewing. From one to three years of age anal satisfaction is the libido's goal. Finally the genitals become the source of pleasure in the phallic stage.

Therapy

Behavioral model
The behavioral model of personality looks at the actions of an individual in order to understand him. There are four types of behavioral therapies. The most used therapy is cognitive behavioral therapy. The focus of cognitive behavioral therapy is to change thought, beliefs or expectations that are associated with psychiatric illness. Modeling therapy is a cognitive behavioral therapy that asks clients to watch people who are using behavior appropriately and then to try it for themselves. Exposure therapy is often used to treat people with phobias. If a person is afraid of spiders for example the counselor may begin therapy by showing him a picture of a fake spider and slowly works up to having him hold a live spider. Flooding is another example of exposure therapy. Last is behavioral modification therapy. In this therapy clients are rewarded for good, adaptive, behavior and/or punished for bad, maladaptive, behavior.

Constructivist psychology
Constructivist therapy works on the premise that counselor and client are equals. Constructivist therapists reject common labels and the notion that there is any one size fits all therapy. The constructivist's job is to help the patient to see how her view of the world is different from actual reality. The client must try to understand the reasons for her emotions and how she can work to incorporate those emotions into a realistic response.

Dialectical behavior therapy
Dialectical behavioral therapy (DBT) was created by Marsha Linehan to treat patients with borderline personality disorder. In DBT clients are given new ways to better cope with their maladaptive behaviors and solve problems on their own. DBT can be used in either group or individual therapy.

Unconscious and archetypes

Carl Jung developed a theory of human development based on Freud's psychodynamic theories though he disagreed with Freud on the definition of the unconscious. Jung proposed that within each individual is the same collective unconscious which contains universal memories. Jung studied art, myths and folklore from around the world and found within them repeating themes which he defined as archetypes. These archetypes are proof of the collective unconscious. One of Jung's lasting contributions to psychology is the idea of extroverted and introverted personality types. Jung defined an extroverted personality as one that is turned outwards to society and introverted as being shy and turned inward. The key to mental health in Jung's view was maintaining a balance between extroversion and introversion.

Human growth and development

Stages

Prenatal stage

The prenatal stage of development begins with conception and ends at the birth of the child. In the past this stage of development was largely ignored due to sciences' ignorance of what went on inside the womb. Prenatal development is further broken down into three distinct stages. The first stage is known as the germinal stage and begins when a sperm cell fertilizes an egg and ends with the implantation of the zygote approximately two weeks later. The embryonic stage then takes over and lasts for another six weeks ending eight weeks after conception. At the end of this stage the embryo is approximately 1 ½ inches long but has already developed eyes, ears, circulatory system, as well as webbed fingers and toes. The final stage, fetal stage, lasts until the baby is born. In this stage the fetus rapidly grows larger and the body systems continue to mature.

Infancy

Infancy begins at birth and lasts until the child's first birthday. Infancy is thought to be one of the most important stages in human development. During this first year infants learn a remarkable number of things. When first born an infant's motor skills consist of grasping and sucking both of which are reflexes. At around three months the child will be able to hold her head up. Most children are sitting without support by the eighth month, crawling by the end of the tenth month and walking with help before their first birthday. Similarly the infant undergoes huge changes in cognitive and emotional development. Infants are born with the instinct to look for human faces and by seven months have developed enough memory to recognize familiar faces. Very early on infants can copy adult facial expressions but the first true smile generally occurs between three or four months of age.

Aging

As the average age of Americans grows older the field of gerontology, study of the aged, grows more important. Ageing affects all aspects of a person both physically and mentally. Wrinkles, gray hair, and a thinner voice are all outward signs of the aging process. Loss of muscle mass and bone density lead to a greater risk of falls, osteoporosis and limited mobility.

All five senses are to some extent affected by aging. Eyesight worsens due to structural changes within the eye. Hearing loss occurs with the cumulative damage to the inner ear. A person's sense of touch decreases and the ability to detect differences in taste and smell declines. While depression does not afflict older people more than younger people it is still important to recognize it when it does occur. Depression not only affects a person's psychological state but can mask or be confused with deeper mental disturbances as well.

Middle childhood

Children are known as toddlers from their first birthday until roughly the age of three when they are begun to be thought of as pre-schoolers. This stage is termed middle childhood. School-age is the term used to define a child who has begun formal schooling but has not yet reached adolescence and is known as late childhood. It is during these stages of human development that children begin to gain a self-identity and sense of independence. Other changes in cognitive development that occur during childhood are the realization that biological gender is permanent regardless of how the child plays or dresses and the knowledge that there is a difference between right and wrong. Parents and other caregivers continue to hold the most important role in the child's development but it is at the age of two or three that the influence of social pressure in the form of playmates begins to arise

Adolescence

Childhood ends and adolescence begins with the onset of puberty. The age of this occurrence is typically between 8 and 13 for girls and 9 and 14 for boys but can vary widely. During this stage of human growth and development peers take on an ever greater role in the child's life as they become more independent.

Adolescence is often marked by great turmoil for the individual as well as the family unit. Hormonal changes within the adolescent's body not only change her physically from child to adult but also create changes in mood and character. Too, they must begin to deal with an ever widening and complex series of problems. They are at a vulnerable stage of moral development which must be recognized by the care-giver. Parents who stay involved in their child's life do have a positive influence on them and forge strong familial bonds.

Adulthood

The age of adulthood is typically defined in legal terms as 18; however, being an adult is largely based on what you are doing rather than a specific age. Unlike the previous stages of development, adulthood is not marked by physical growth but by personal growth. The phases in adulthood are marked by specific milestones. Early adulthood is typically the time when a person leaves home and begins to support themselves. Often they marry and start a family of their own. Middle adulthood is sometimes characterized as beginning with a mid-life crisis. It is at this time that adults realize that the life they are living is their real life and that they will not live forever. Late adulthood typically involves more transitions including retirement, children leaving home and sometimes the death of a spouse. Biologically late adulthood is characterized for women as the onset of menopause.

Stages of development

Fetal growth and development

Infectious diseases such as rubella can have a profoundly negative affect on the fetus if the mother contracts it during her first four weeks of pregnancy. Other diseases which cross over the placental blood barrier include chicken pox, malaria and tuberculosis. AIDS and genital herpes can infect the child at birth due to the exchange of fluids during the birthing process.

Substances such as cocaine and alcohol have an extremely harmful affect on the baby. Children born of mothers who used cocaine during pregnancy are often born addicted to it and will show a large number of birth defects such as heart malformations and brain lesions. It has been shown that the binge drinking of alcohol can leave a child born with fetal alcohol syndrome which causes both physical and mental disabilities. Smoking while pregnant can cause the baby to be of low birth rate and also leads to an increase of miscarriage and stillbirth.

Sensorimotor stage of development

Piaget defined the first stage of human cognitive development, sensorimotor, as beginning with birth and lasting until the 24 month. Piaget believed that babies only relate to the outside world through motor capabilities and by things they can physically hear, see, smell, taste or touch. They cannot actively think about the world or use mental images to relate to it. However, by the age of eight or nine months children will obtain the ability to realize that objects exist even when they cannot be seen known as object permanence. Recent studies show that Piaget vastly underestimated the mind of infants.

Preoperational stage of development

The preoperational stage, which begins around a child's 24 month and lasts until the age of seven is Piaget's second stage of cognitive development. In this stage Piaget believed that children were unable to see the world from someone else's point of view, he called this egocentrism. Children begin to engage in imaginary play and begin to play with other children rather than always playing alone during this time. Piaget also believed that children in this stage could not have rational thoughts and lacked an understanding of the principle of conservation. Because Piaget only tested a small number of children on a single task he probably did not realize the extent to which young children can actually perform these behaviors.

Concrete operations stage of development

Piaget stated that logical thought begins to be shown by children sometime after the age of six or seven. While this concrete operations stage typically lasts until the child is eleven years old most people operate within this stage of thinking nearly all the time. Children are now able to view situations from perspectives other than their own. The ability to understand conservation is another hallmark of this stage. Previously a child would not understand that volume remains the same regardless of the shape or size of the container, now though they realize that volume is permanent and doesn't change with shape. Also the idea that certain actions can be reversed begins in this stage of cognitive development.

Formal operations stage of development

Piaget felt that at about the age of twelve and with the onset of adolescence children enter the formal operations stage of reasoning and cognitive development. Abstract thought emerges in this stage and allows the adolescent to form and test ideas that are not concrete such as ides on the topics of religion, morality and relationships between people. Also they begin to be able to test questions from more than one viewpoint. There is some controversy as to whether all people reach this stage of reasoning. Even those who do reach this stage however do not rely on it solely but usually use concrete operations to find answers to the questions and problems of daily life.

Information-processing perspective of cognitive development

The information-processing perspective looks at several different factors in regards to human cognitive development however, unlike many cognitive development theories it disregards the environment and focuses wholly on the internal processes. This theory takes its inspiration from computer processing models. Attention is one factor that affects the thought process. As children age they develop longer attention spans and with this the ability to study longer and stay focused longer enabling them to learn more. Also as children develop cognitively they acquire new methods of memorization which in turn increases their ability to learn. Metacognition, the ability to realize how one is thinking allows the child to develop better strategies of thought for specific situations and to change strategies when one no longer works.

Erik Erikson's course of development

Erikson named his approach to development, psychosocial, and believed that people are influenced by both biological and social factors. Erikson's theory consisted of eight distinct stages that a person passes through during a lifetime of development.

Trust versus mistrust, stage one, begins with birth and lasts until an infant's first birthday. The second stage is marked by autonomy versus shame. The balance between initiative and guilt marks the third stage. The school age child experiences stage four as a crisis of competence versus inferiority. Identity versus role confusion occurs alongside puberty and is the fifth stage. The sixth stage is intimacy versus isolation and occurs during young adulthood. In middle adulthood the seventh stage, generativity versus stagnation, appears. The final stage ego integrity versus despair happens as an individual ages. Erikson believed that mental illness was caused by a person stagnating in one stage unable to develop further or when an individual swung too heavily to one extreme of a stage or the other.

Behavioral theories of human development

Unlike psychodynamic theories which focus on inner thoughts, behavioral theories focus on directly observable behavior and believe the environment plays an important role in development. John Watson and B.F. Skinner founded this movement on the idea that development is continuous throughout the life span and does not come in distinct stages. Through experimentation they showed that most learning comes from the child's surroundings, nurture, instead of from their genes, nature. Albert Bandura worked on the social learning theory and was a very important researcher in the field of behavioral development. Bandura showed that children learn most easily from watching other people. In a now classic experiment he allowed children to play with a toy clown. Afterwards he had the children to watch a video of an adult striking the toy clown behaving roughly with it, then allowed the children to play with the clown again. The children were almost always more violent with the clown after viewing the video than before.

Nature versus nurture

Psychologists have long sought to solve the problem of nature versus nurture. Nature is defined as the genetics with which one is born. Nature is set and unchangeable. Nurture is defined as the environment in which a person is raised and develops. Nurture is different for every single individual including identical twins, as no one can have exactly the same experiences as someone else. Some psychologists believe that personality is influenced entirely by nature. They would argue that personality is set at conception and cannot be changed regardless of the environment in which a person develops. Other psychologists argue that genetics have nothing to do with personality. They would say that people are born "blank slates" upon which personality is written by nurture. Most psychologist today fall somewhere along the line of continuum between 100% nature and 100% nurture.

Karen Horney personality development

Karen Horney's model of personality development stressed that a person cannot be studied out of context to her environment and culture. Horney's model was in direct conflict with her mentor's, Freud, emphasis on sexual trauma. Horney emphasized that children must have more than just their biological needs met. She felt that children who are not brought up with warmth and love become hostile and either directs this hostility out at the world or inward at themselves. The result of this hostility is psychological disorders. Horney also defined three ways in which people associate with other people. First, they can move toward the other looking for love for example. Second, they can move away from others in an attempt to express independence. Last, they can move against others in conflict or anger.

Ego

Sometimes, Freud proposed, the things the id desires are in direct conflict with reality and the ego must use defense mechanisms in order to protect itself. Anna Freud developed a list of seven common defense mechanisms. Repression blocks harmful ideas, emotions or memories from the conscious mind. Projection lets the ego place personal feelings onto someone else. Feelings which produce unconscious anxiety are changed into good feelings in the conscious mind by the reaction formation. Regression occurs when a person becomes anxious moving from one stage to another and allows the person to remain in the lower more comfortable stage. The refusal to admit to bad feelings or events is denial. Displacement occurs when a person becomes angry at someone or something that is not the actual object of their anger. Intellectualization and rationalization are higher level defense mechanisms which rely on thinking.

Reinforcement and punishment

There are two types of reinforcers and punishers, primary and secondary. Primary reinforcers are things which satisfy a basic need such as food or water. Primary punishers such as extreme heat or cold are very powerful. Secondary reinforcers, a smile, good grades, and punishers, a frown, bad grades are learned.

Another way to categorize reinforcers and punishers is into positive and negative sets. The following chart explains these sets.

Procedure	Nature of Stimulus	Type of Event	Effect on Response
Positive Reinforcement	Pleasant	Stimulus presented	Increases
Negative Reinforcement	Aversive	Stimulus removed	Increases

Negative Punishment/Pleasant/Stimulus removed/Decreases

Positive Punishment/Aversive/Stimulus presented/Decreases

Narcissistic and dependent personality disorders

Narcissism is established by early adulthood. It is characterized by at least five of the following symptoms:
- belief that they are better than everyone else
- wishes for the ultimate in all aspirations
- belief that they can only associate with other "special" people
- needs more praise than normal
- thinks that they are owed something just for being themselves
- uses other people to get what they want
- unable to empathize
- thinks people are envious of them
- haughty behaviors.

Dependent personality disorder is described as extremely needy behavior. The individual with dependent personality disorder will do anything to have someone take care of them. The DSM-IV-TR requires that five or more of the following symptoms be observed:
- needs help making day to day decisions
- cannot assume responsibility for their own life
- does not like to express opposite opinions for fear of being abandoned
- lacks the self-confidence to start tasks without direction
- takes extreme measures to win approval
- dislikes being alone
- moves from one serious relationship to another
- is extremely afraid of having to care for themselves.

Family Functioning

The old saying that families come in all shapes and sizes is truer today than ever before. One hundred years ago the average American family home contained several generations living together. Fifty years ago the average family in America was made up of a husband, his wife and their children. Thirty years ago the rising divorce rate added two more family structures to the American way of life, the single parent home and the blended family (including step-parents and step-children). In today's ever diversifying world it is important to recognize several other types of families as well: dual-income families, childless families, gay or lesbian families and multicultural families. Each type of family demands a unique perspective in the counseling situation.

Family life cycle

Just as individual humans grow and develop so do families. There are generally nine recognized stages to the family life cycle. The first stage of a new family begins when a young adult leaves the family she grew up with. Getting married and having children mark the second and third stages. The next three stages deal specifically with child rearing encompassing the preschool-age, school-age and teenage child. Each of the child rearing stages has its own unique problems and joys. The seventh stage is known as the launching center because the family's role at this time is to enable older children to leave and begin their own family. Middle age, stage eight, is when a couple must re-form a close relationship with one another. The final stage of the family life cycle, retirement, requires the nurturing of the third generation and dealing with the death of a spouse.

Circumplex model

David Olson developed the circumplex model of marital and family systems in which he described two dimensions, family cohesion and family adaptability. Family cohesion is defined as the aspect of emotional bonding that occurs among family members. The second dimension, family adaptability, concerns the family's ability to change and stay flexible through out changes in the family life cycle. Both dimensions have four levels of functionality. Family cohesion is measured from low to high, in terms of disengaged, separated, connected and enmeshed. Family adaptability is measured from low to high, in terms of rigid, structured, flexible and chaotic. The family unit must find balance on both dimensions in order to function healthily. Balanced families are either flexibly separated, flexibly connected, structurally separated or structurally connected. Each family must be measured individually because their stage in the family life cycle and makeup must be taken into account when using the circumplex model.

Maggie Scarf

Scarf studied family patterns and organized a continuum on which family functioning exists. On the low end of the continuum is the family that is "severely disturbed", here there is no one in control or in a position of leadership. Families which are inflexible and which see everything as either all bad or all good are at level two. Level three consists of family members that each try to wield control by withholding love until other members act as they wish. The most successful type of family has a secure center and an attitude of responsibility toward each other. The healthier the family is then the better off mentally are its members. Healthy families hold on to one another tightly but know when to let go and allow each other to move successfully through the developmental cycle.

Family system

- Interdependence. The idea that a family cannot be understood by looking at individual members.
- Subsystems are the smaller units, husband and wife for example, within the larger system.
- Circularity refers to the fact that cause and effect are impossible to determine as every individual effects another in a chain reaction.
- Equifinality is the realization that there is no single best way to family health, a specific plan for each family must be created.
- Communication. Without communication no system can function properly.
- Family rules must be determined for each family.
- Once a family has reached a good level of functioning it must be maintained by homeostasis.

The concept of morphogenesis states that families must remain flexible in order to adapt to change.

Communication

There are six important facets to good family communication. The first important feature is, communicate often. Even if you have to schedule time in your busy day, make time to talk. Particularly important during times of conflict is the need to communicate clearly and directly. Third, be an active listener. Try to understand the problem from the speaker's point of view and ask questions if you don't understand something completely. Because each family member is different it is important to always keep in mind the person with whom you are talking to. This fourth feature is especially important when adults communicate with children. Fifth, pay attention to non-verbal cures. Non-verbal communication includes facial expressions and body stance and adds a deeper layer of understanding to conversation. Last, stay positive. It is sometimes easy to feel that family problems are overwhelming and unsolvable but keeping a positive outlook will vastly improve overall communication.

Issues of Diversity

ADRESSING model of culture

Hayes developed the ADRESSING model of culture which has nine cultural factors, related minority groups and biases. "A" stands for age, its minority group is older adults. Bias against older adults is known as ageism. "D" is for disability which includes anyone with a disability and discrimination against them. "R" represents religion. The main religious minorities in America are Jews and Muslims, bias against these two groups is known as anti-Semitism. "E" includes ethnicity and race. Ethnic and racial minorities in America include African Americans, Asian Americans and Latinos. Prejudice against racial minorities is called racism. The first "S" in ADRESSING represents social status. People who are poor or uneducated make up the social minorities. Classism is bias against these people. The second "S" stands for sexual orientation. Prejudice against homosexuals is called heterosexism. Another form of racism is towards indigenous peoples which is what "I" stands for. Racism and colonialism are biases towards anyone who is a refugee, immigrant or international student. "N" stands for national origin. The final letter "G" represents gender. Women are the minority group and sexism is discrimination against them.

Culture

Axelson gave the broadest definition of culture as, "any group of people who identify or associate with one another on the basis of some common purpose, need or similarity of background." Sometimes people associate culture with how one looks are what one eats but generally the most important thing that people within a culture share is a common history. Another formal definition of culture is based on ethnographic information for example religion or language. Similarly, demographic information such as age or gender may tie people to a particular culture. Last, status variables, also known as socio-economic factors are sometimes used to define a specific culture. These variables include financial and educational background. The American Heritage Dictionary defines culture as "the totality of socially transmitted behavior patterns, arts, beliefs, institutions, and all other products of human work and thought."

Understanding culture

The Association for Multicultural Counseling and Development uses three issues in their guide to multicultural counseling. First, a counselor must be learned in the worldview of their client. Second, a counselor must understand his own worldview. Third, a counselor must have or obtain skills for working with clients from different cultures. Another model used in multicultural counseling is the idea that they find important before choosing a theory for the client. Cultural bias may also make for difficulties between counselor and client. The McFadden model may be used in helping to overcome cultural bias. The model asks counselors to understand many cultures from a cultural-historical, psychosocial, and scientific-ideological viewpoint. Counselors who are best able to relate to certain cultures should be most referred to those particular clients so that client and counselor can receive the highest benefit.

Multicultural counseling

There are two ways to view multicultural counseling: the ethic view places the importance on what people have in common; the emic view asks that counseling be tailored to a particular culture and client. Whichever method is used there are several difficulties in multicultural counseling. First is that people often assume that reactions to poverty or discrimination is a form of culture, this mistake is known as overculturalizing. The second way to view multicultural counseling is the problem of language. Counselors may be asked to work with clients who speak English as second language, when this occurs counselors must make sure that the client understands everything fully. Clients who come from a minority background may also be dealing with racism. The counselor must try to help the client respond to racism in ways that are proactive. Lastly, is the problem of acculturation. Acculturation is the process of becoming more like the people in the majority while giving up old patterns of behavior. This can be a difficult and stressful process that the counselor can help with.

Good services difficulty in multicultural counseling

Sue proposed that multicultural counseling should be formed on the basis of understanding the client's internal and external feelings of control and responsibility. Sue also devised five ideas for making counseling across cultures easier. First, counselors must recognize what they believe are good behaviors for people. Second, counselors must recognize that psychological and social theories are not cultural free. Each theory is influenced by the culture in which it was formed. Third, counselor must be able to understand that personality is influenced by the environment in which a person lives. Fourth, counselors should be able to recognize the client's worldview as being acceptable even though it may differ from their own. Fifth, counselors must use many different theories, techniques, and skills to best serve their clients because no one set of ideas will work for all clients.

Ethics and values in multicultural counseling

Working with multicultural clients can cause ethical conflicts for counselors because the values of their clients can vary significantly from their own. Counselors must realize that ethics and values stem from culture and therefore may change from client to client. Because counselors must be supportive of the client's ethics they must educate themselves to the cultural background of the client. However, it must be understand that oppression and cruelty are not to be accepted as proper behavior regardless of the client's cultural views on these topics.

Culture also affects the way in which people react to problems and ask for help. Knowing the cultural norms within the community that the counselor works is very important for implementing proper individual and community services. Counselors must remain neutral in what they believe to be culturally appropriate or not. Counselors must also remain unbiased and maintain a respect for diversity.

Cross-cultural knowledge and cross-cultural leadership in multicultural counseling

Cross-cultural knowledge is necessary for effective multicultural counseling. Cross-cultural knowledge refers to specific knowledge of the cultural background of their clients including, history, customs and practices. It is also the realization that traditional theories of psychology may not fit a diverse population of clients. Continuing education is necessary for the multicultural counselor because culture is ever changing. Cross-cultural leadership refers to several factors both within the field of social work as well as in society at large. Within the field of social work multicultural counselors must undertake the responsibility to develop new theories of behavior and therapies that apply to a multicultural population. A multicultural counselor must be able to explain their client base in positive terms in order to further the acceptance and tolerance of the clients by other groups. Multicultural counselors must also act as advocates for their clients' concerns. The counselor must become the voice of the people they represent.

Skills of multicultural counselors

Multicultural counselors must have many skills for working with their clients. They must be able to work with people who are congruous and people who are disparate from them in terms of culture. Also they must learn what culture means to their clients and keep an open dialogue regarding culturally influenced behavior. Counselors should be able to understand the difficulties faced when dealing with clients who speak English as a second language. They must make cultural assessments and then plan treatment around these assessments. Talking with supervisors and colleagues about how they are doing is important as well. They should be aware of and refer to community resources important to the client's culture. Multicultural counselors must take on the role of leader and advocate on their client's behalf.

Language with multicultural clients

Language is an important part of culture and personal identity. If a client speaks English as a second language the social worker must be sure that they understand all verbal and written instructions fully. When clients have little or no English language skills the social worker should provide literature and services to them in their native language. There are several ways to accomplish this task. First, the social worker may hire a staff member fluent in the language that a majority of clients use. The staff member would be expected translate literature as well as act as an interpreter therefore they should be trained professionals who have had instruction in the ethics of social work practice. Another option is to make use of a community sponsored language professional. These people will have had special training for being a liaison in the cultural community. If neither of the above options is feasible the social worker must seek out other competent social workers who are able to deal with language issues and refer their clients to them.

Referring clients

Social workers should keep up to date on the diverse cultural resources within their community and beyond. They should also be sure that minorities are not being excluded or under-represented from resources. Within their practice social workers must make an effort to provide clients with visible evidence of their commitment to multiculturalism. There are several ways that social workers can work towards accomplishing the goal of multiculturalism at all levels of their own practice and society. First, they can hire staff from a variety of backgrounds and cultures and those with knowledge of the issues of diversity. Second, they can try to find service models that fit their clients and advocate research for more multicultural models. Third, they should be sure that any decorations within the practice reflect the client base. Fourth, they must never allow staff remarks that insult or put down clients or their culture. Last, they should consult with the community for in-put in new and necessary services as well as for feedback on services already in place.

Culturagram

Elaine P. Congress developed a culturagram to help further the social worker's proficiency in working with multicultural clients. Below is her chart which indicates that all of the issues are equally important.

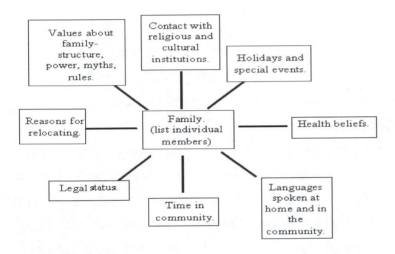

Multicultural marriage counseling

Counseling a multicultural couple has unique problems separate from the normal problems of marriage counseling. While the number of multicultural couples in America is far greater than ever before there are still many stereotypes involved that the couple will come across when dealing with other people. It is important for the social worker to note these stereotypes and help the clients handle this issue in a proactive way. Some of these stereotypes include the belief that a person who marries outside of his/her culture does so for personal gain, rebellion against their own culture or society, and low self-esteem. Multicultural couples often struggle with the process of keeping their own cultural heritage alive while respecting the cultural values of their spouse. The process becomes even more complex when children are involved as the couple must make decisions on child rearing. Other cultural problems involve religion, gender roles and the role of extended family members.

Problems in counseling multiracial individuals

Multiracial individuals suffer from the fact that it is difficult to find images of themselves in media and literature. Problems that are often dealt with by multiracial individuals must be understood by the social worker in order to help the client cope. Sometimes it is hard to be different from mainstream society; multiracial people face the problem of uniqueness every day. Multiracial clients may also feel that they do not fit into a specific racial group causing issues with acceptance and belonging. Physical appearance can be especially problematic for multiracial women as they try to fit themselves into the societal norms for beauty. Also important to multiracial women is that they are judged by how the look bringing to the fore sexual stereotyping. Self-esteem is impacted by the factors already noted as well as others. It is important for the social worker to help multiracial clients develop a strong sense of self and self-worth.

Multiracial children and adolescents

Problems facing multiracial individuals differ according to their age and stage of development. Social workers counseling multiracial children must be sure that the child is being exposed to ideas that represent many different cultures and races so that they might learn that everyone is unique in their own special way and that there is nothing wrong about being multiracial. It is also important to help the family maintain a stable relationship that allows the child to investigate all facets of their heritage.

Adolescence is difficult for everyone but may be more acutely problematic for those who are multiracial. In this stage of development children are most concerned with fitting in. Because they do not look like their peers they may feel pressure to conform in other ways. This may also be the time when they first encounter racism making it difficult to form a positive self identity.

Assessment, Diagnosis and Intervention Planning

Social history

Initial intake interview

There are a number of things which must be established during an initial intake interview.

- The client's primary information: name, phone number, address, how old they are, male or female, whether or not they are married and what they do for a living.
- Learn why they are coming for counseling and how these issues are affecting their life.
- Briefly define how the client spends free time and ask them to go over an average day.
- Obtain information about their parents, siblings, family medical history and family functioning.
- Determine a personal history for the following: illnesses and hospitalizations, educations, if they served in the military, work, intercourse, marriage and prior counseling.
- Ask what their goals are for counseling and life.
- Note the client's nonverbal behavior, how they look, basic level of intelligence and abnormal behavior.

Make an overview of the interview including how it went, how you can best help the client and whether or not the client is ready to participate in meaningful counseling.

Use of assessment instruments

Forms of assessment

There are seven widely used forms of assessment in social psychology. Standard assessment uses a test that has been normalized for a large number of people and compares and individual's score to the norm for his age or grade level. Alternative assessment is used to see the individual's thought process or ability to make something. Self assessment asks the individual to take note of how he is doing. Placement assessment is typically used in education and business and determines whether a person is ready to be promoted to the next level. Diagnostic assessment looks at what a person is good at and what they need further instruction in. Formative assessment, the portfolio for example, is an ongoing process that reassures the individual as they work. Summative assessments are tests used at the end of a specified length of time.

Behavioral assessment

Behavioral assessments wish to measure or identify things that a person does or thinks in response to specific stimuli. The triple-response system is used for the assessment and treatment of the patient. Organismic variables are anything that has an effect on the patient including medical conditions, genes and the amount of time spent working on the observed task. Response variables are what the person does when presented with the stimulus. These behaviors can be motor, physiological or emotional. Motor responses to a stimulus are the physical actions the patient makes. Physiological behaviors are observable only with help such as listening to the heart rate with a stethoscope. Self report is used for emotional responses. Consequent variables include rewards and punishments and help to decide whether behaviors will be repeated. These assessments are used to help a person change unwanted actions or acquire new behaviors.

Clinical interview process

The clinical interview is a very popular form of assessment because it allows the clinician to gather both verbal answers to questions and nonverbal responses to the surrounding environment. There are many things that can be accomplished in the clinical interview form. First, the interviewer can ascertain the person's level of consciousness by observing her directly. Second, interviews build trust and understanding between the social worker and the client. Also interviews can be used to evaluate an ongoing treatment program or talk about follow-up procedures. Clinical interviews do have some drawbacks, however. If the environment is noisy, completely unfamiliar to the client, or in some way threatening to her answers will be distorted or untrue. Because responses made during interviews are subjective, different clinicians may interpret the same answers differently.

Self-report assessment

Self-report assessments are generally in the form of a question sheet which the client fills out in private. These questions may be open ended, "How are you feeling today?" for example, multiple choice, "I'm feeling ___happy ___sad ___angry today.", or scaled, "Place a mark on the scale that represents how you are feeling today very happy---------happy-------neutral------- sad-------very sad." Self-reports are easy for the client to take but they can be highly inaccurate. Some clients may try to guess the "right" answer, what they think the clinician wants to hear, or may lie in an attempt to change their true condition. Self-reports can be used in a variety of settings including one-on-one, group, schools, and jobs. Also this type of assessment can be written to measure a number of different things including personality, depression, intelligence, and satisfaction.

Tests

Ability and intelligence tests

Alfred Binet first introduced the term "intelligence quotient" or IQ and defined it as the ratio of mental age to chronological age. The long standing Stanford-Binet IQ test was first developed in 1916 and is the model for many other intelligence tests today. The Wechsler scale measures both verbal and performance intelligence and has different exams for children and adults. In the field of psychometrics specific abilities rather than overall intelligence is the focus. Phillip Vernon and Raymond Cattell described two types of abilities, fluid, reasoning and problem solving, and crystallized, such as vocabulary. There are three widely used ability tests: SCAT, STEP and SAT. The SCAT, School and College Ability Test, is most concerned about aptitude in verbal and quantitative categories. The STEP, Sequential Tests of Educational Progress, records the skills students have learned in reading, written language and math. The SAT, Scholastic Aptitude Test, measure a student's readiness for college level work and overall intelligence.

COPS

The Career Occupational Preference System (COPS) was first developed by multiple-factor analysis in 1968 but has been updated and translated into many languages since then. The COPS lists 168 work related activities and asks participants to respond how much they like doing them on a scale form very much to dislike very much. Careers for each job type are split between "professional", usually requiring a bachelor's degree and "skilled", jobs in which people are trained for specific tasks. The job types listed are science, technology, consumer economics, outdoor, business, arts and service. This assessment is most widely used in middle/high schools and colleges. It is meant to get adolescents and young adults to think about various career possibilities rather than give one perfect option.

Kuder Occupational Interest Survey

The Kuder Occupational Interest Survey (KIOS) was originally published in 1939. The latest version was designed for middle/high school students. The areas of interest looked at for on the KIOS are outdoor, mechanical, computational, scientific, persuasive, artistic, literary, musical, social science and clerical. The results are compared with the results for people in jobs where they are happy and with college students' choice of major. This type of result gives the child an overview of what types of jobs they might most enjoy. The results can be used by the individual themselves are with the help of a guidance counselor or other adult. The KIOS is now available in pencil and paper format as well as a computer based format. The older a person is when completing this exam the more reliable the results are.

Strong Interest Inventory and the General Aptitude Test Battery

The Strong Interest Inventory is used as an assessment tool for students who may wish to enter college. It was created by E. K. Strong, Jr. after over twenty years of research. An individual wishing to take the Strong Interest Inventory should be at least 13 and have a sixth grade reading level. It takes about 30 minutes to finish the 325 entries about things they like to do.

The General Aptitude Test Battery (GATB) is used to match people with jobs that they would be good at. There are two sections on this test hands-on and paper-and-pencil. The hands-on section asks the individual to complete motor activities and measures finger dexterity for example. The paper-and-pencil has questions on verbal and mathematical concepts.

HTP test

The House-Tree-Person (HTP) is a projective assessment which asks the individual to draw houses, trees and people in an effort to gain insight into the individual's personality. This test can also be used as an assessment of brain functioning. While there are several variations in the most basic form of the HTP the trained administrator first asks the individual to draw the pictures on separate pieces of paper one at a time using a crayon. Next the examiner asks sixty questions about each drawing for example, "Is the tree alive." Sometimes the examiner asks the individual to draw all the pictures on a single sheet of paper for a look at their relationship toward one another. There are two separate ways to evaluate the outcome of the HTP. When used to measure intelligence the drawings are looked at objectively to see how much detail the drawer has put into each one. Used in this manner the score correlates well with actual I.Q. However, the drawings may also be looked at subjectively to test for personality disorders, but with low reliability and validity.

Mental status exam

The mental status exam is used to evaluate an individual on first meeting and is often used during crisis situations to ascertain the level of threat the individual might be. The majority of the exam is done by observing the individual and takes at most five minutes to complete. First noted is the outward looks of the individual including gender, age, height, etc, also how the person is dressed and whether they seem taken care of. Next as they come into the room note how they walk, hold themselves and move their hands. Be aware of their mood and demeanor. In regards to language are they able to speak and understand well? Check their short and long term memory, orientation to time and place and whether they are alert. By asking questions about recent history, simple mathematics, favorite movie and the meaning of simple proverbs assess their level of intelligence, concentration, thought process and possibility of delusional thinking. Also note their level of tension, emotional/nonverbal responses, whether they appear at risk of harming themselves or others, if they appear to have been abused and possible defense mechanisms used to avoid certain topics.

Projective tests

Personality assessment can be done in the form of projective tests such as the Draw-a-Tree, TAT, and Rorschach. These assessments use the interpretation of an individual's answers to try to determine what sort of person they are. Each person will answer in a unique way so these are the opposite of "standardized" tests. Also each therapist has much leeway in reading the answers so that the same results may lead to different outcomes based on the therapist. The Rorschach test is the most famous projective test developed by Hermann Rorschach in 1921 and was revised by five different American psychologists according to their theoretical beliefs. In this test individuals are shown a series of cards on which inkblots have been printed. The therapist writes down exactly what the person says and does when given the card. Half of the cards are black and white, three have pastel colors and two have a small amount of red.

Psychological tests

Psychological tests help the counselor to quantify the client's behavior, personality or disorder. In order to correctly administer, interpret and apply the results the counselor must study the test in depth and know the following information about it: what individuals were used to norm the test, how well do the test results hold up over time, how well do scores hold up from one administration to the next involving the same individual, how does this test compare to similar methods of assessment, how the test is scored, what is the proper procedure for giving the test, what is the test designed to measure, and what are the test's weaknesses. Counselors who use one or two tests quite frequently should produce statistics in regards to their local area and client base. This information will be more applicable than national statistics. If a counselor is unfamiliar with a test they need to use they may want to bring in a testing specialist to administer it.

Tests

There are many arguments for and against the use of tests in counseling. Major arguments against testing are:

- testing makes the client less likely to volunteer information and the counselor is less likely to seek information using other means
- test results interfere with the counselor's true impression of the client
- test results do not hold up well enough over time to be trusted
- tests are often biased against large sets of people
- tests are easy to trick and lie on.

Arguments for tests include:

- tests give quick results in an easy non-threatening manner
- test results are easy for both counselor and client to understand and make use of
- tests can be used to guide individuals in career options
- tests allow counselor and clients to see how the therapy is or isn't working.

Test validity

Good tests have high validity and reliability, are well standardized and normed accurately. Validity is defined as how well a test assesses what it is supposed to assess. Validity comes in four different types. Construct validity is usually in reference to inventories that measure personality or interest. Construct validity is how well an item on the test which was designed

- 33 -

to relate to a specific attribute actually relates to that attribute. Criterion validity is a measure of how well the test's results hold up over time. Content or face validity looks at how well the entire test does in achieving its professed goals. Consequential validity refers to what effect the knowledge of the test results may have on the client.

Test reliability, standardization and norms

Reliability is how well scores hold up from one administration to the next of the same test to the same individual Reliability may be checked by using

- test-retest, the exact same test is given to the individual twice within some measure of time
- alternate-form, if the assessment has more than one version the client is given each version in turn
- internal consistency analysis, the assessment questions on the test are placed in two groups and the scores in each group are compared.

Standardization means that the way in which a test is given must be the same every time. For example if the test is timed to 50 minutes no one should be allowed more than 50 minutes on the exam for any reason. Accurate norms allow for an individual's score to be compared with the average score on that test. Tests should be normed using a variety of individuals.

Test administration

Because each test is administered differently how a test should be administered is typically spelt out in the manual that comes with a particular test. Even versions of the same test may have different policies and procedures for administration so it is important to become familiar with the administration of commonly used tests. Administration instructions should include the number of people who can be tested at one time (individually or groups), the location for testing (office, class room, home), time limits or lack thereof, forms of help available to the test taker during the exam (verbal help from administrator, dictionary, textbook, calculator, etc), the physical and developmental age that the test is appropriate for and whether or not the test taker should have a choice in which test to take. This last instruction is often not found in the manual but may be guided by whether or not choosing their own test will be beneficial to the client, if it will help them accept the results and whether or not choice of test will lead to a better understanding of the client by the counselor.

Test interpretation

Tests can generally be interpreted in one of four ways. First, is a descriptive interpretation. This interpretation gives the most basic understanding of a score as in an IQ score of 110 means the individual is of slightly above average intelligence. Genetic interpretation allows the counselor to explain how the individual came to have the score. For example a counselor may tell a client who scores high on a scale of aggression that they became aggressive due in part to witnessing abuse during childhood. Predictive interpretation is used to try to learn how the client will behave in the future; this type of interpretation is particularly useful on interest inventories were the counselor aims to guide the client into educational or career opportunities that the client will enjoy or perform well at. Evaluative interpretation allows the counselor to make recommendations to the client. Designing a course of therapy is one way in which evaluative interpretation is used.

Problems of test interpretation

There are several ways in which test interpretation can be problematic. First, the interpreter may not have the proper knowledge or education needed to interpret the test correctly. By taking classes on specific interpretations allowing more qualified individuals to interpret results and by becoming particularly efficient in only the tests normally used this problem can be diminished. Next, scores must not be taken out of context. The general evaluation of a client is more informative than a single test score which can be influenced by many contradictory variables. Also a better way to interpret scores is based on percentile ranking rather than raw score. Test interpretation must be thought out and planned. The counselor should go over the test results in private, writing out his thoughts and observations and researching ideas when necessary. The counselor should explain to the client why the particular test was used, what the results are and then ask the client what she feels the score means guiding were necessary. One way to help a client understand the results is to present them in graphic form.

MBTI

The Myers-Briggs Type Indicator (MBTI) is a very popular personality test because it is easy to take and score and the interpretation is built in to the outcome. The MBTI was developed on the personality theories of Carl Jung who believed that every person has a set way of going about daily life and handling problems. The results of the MBTI are expressed in a four letter code which refers to the four characteristics that make up an individual's personality. The way that these characteristics interact is known as type dynamics. The dominant characteristic is the one that is the strongest part of the personality makeup. It influences all of the other characteristics and everything that an individual does. The auxiliary characteristic helps the dominant one by adding harmony. The MBTI is made up of 144 items, takes approximately 2 hours to complete and is empirically keyed. It can be taken by adolescents, young adults, adults and older adults. The various types of the MBTI may be used for the assessment of learning style, social skills, and career counseling.

MBTI types introverted, extroverted, sensing and intuition

There are eight personality types measured along four separate continuums on the Myers-Briggs Type Indicator (MBTI). The first set is introvert-extrovert. This set defines how an individual relates to the outside world and how he obtains energy. The introverted individual prefers to be alone and is often seen as shy and quiet. The extroverted individual likes to be around people and may be described as outgoing. The second set of characteristics is sensing-intuition. This set measures the way that an individual likes to learn and process information. The individual who falls closer to the sensing side of the continuum likes to gain information through their five-senses. They like to learn by doing and are sometimes thought of as "hands-on" learners. An intuitive individual would rather make connections using the mind.

MBTI types thinking, feeling, judging and perceiving

There are eight personality types measured along four separate continuums on the Myers-Briggs Type Indicator (MBTI) including the thinking-feeling set and the judging-perceiving set. An individual's decision making is influenced by the thinking-feeling set of characteristics. Those individual's that lie on the thinking side of the continuum tend to be more logical wishing to use information to solve problems and make decisions. On the other side of the continuum is the feeling personality which relies very heavily on emotion rather than reason to make decisions.

How an individual behaves in and reacts to the world outside the mind is determined by the judging-perceiving set of personality characteristics. Judging does not refer to how the individual appraises others but rather how they go about their daily life. Individuals who are judging are more likely to look at life from the parts to the whole perspective and plan their activities carefully. Those individuals classified as perceiving tend to being with the whole and then break it down into parts for better understanding and are more "take it as it comes" in concerns with scheduling.

Inventories

Interest inventories

Interest inventories concern themselves only with what a person likes or thinks they might like to do. They do not ascertain the person's ability to do the task. The development of interest inventories can occur in two ways or in a combination of both. Empirically based inventories are created by giving the survey to large numbers of people in particular careers; the answers they give are used to make clusters of items that point to certain job fields. Theory based inventories are created according to theoretical ideas. *Making Vocational Choices: A Theory of Careers* by John L. Holland is a popular theory that has had several interest inventories created with its ideas. Holland's theory involves six job categories: "realistic, investigative, artistic, social, enterprising, and conventional."

Interest inventories typically use one of two methods of obtaining the information. One such method is to ask the person to pick one answer from two or more choices. The format might be look like: (1) I like _____ best. a. biology b. art c. reading. Another method is to ask how much they like or dislike certain activities or jobs. For example: (1) painting a house ___enjoy very much ____enjoy a little ____ neutral ____dislike a little ____dislike very much.

Interest inventories are usually created to help young people make decisions about educational and career questions. They may be designed for many different types of jobs or for a particular type of job by an agency looking for new workers.

MCMI

The Millon Clinical Multiaxial Inventory (MCMI) is a short assessment of personality based on the theories of Dr. Millon as well as years of empirical data. The test looks at both Axis I and Axis II of the DSM-IV-TR. It is available in different forms for children, adolescents and adults.

The only requirements for the adult exam are that the individual have an eight grade reading level and 25-30 minutes. There are 14 personality disorder scales made up of 11 moderate and 3 severe personality disorders. There are also 10 clinical syndrome scales made up of 7 moderate and 3 severe syndromes; as well as a correction scale measuring validity. The MCMI is particularly useful in institutional situation such as hospitals and prisons where it can be given to large groups and scored via a computer system.

WOWI

The World of Work Inventory (WOWI) is a test which was developed to assist young adults in their career decision choices. The individual's score leads to a list of jobs that they have both the aptitude and interest for. The WOWI is made up of five parts which take approximately an hour to complete and can be filled out on a computer or paper-and-pencil. The first section is simply the individual's identifying information. The second part asks the individual to pick two jobs she thinks she might like to do and her two favorite areas in school. The remainder of the exam has a total of 330 items. On the career interest activities part the individual selects whether she likes, dislikes, or feels neutral towards a list of things done at a number of different jobs. The training potentials part of the exam tests whether the individual has the ability to perform the work demanded from various jobs. The final part, job satisfaction indicators, match the individual's personality with jobs they would be happiest and most fulfilled by.

Problem identification

Addictive personality and behaviors

Some personality traits linked to substance addiction include low self-esteem, easily frustrated, being unable to control impulses, and rigid thinking. People can be addicted to a wide number of things and sometimes give up one addiction only to pick up another. Common addictions include sex, work, alcohol and drugs. The DSM-IV-TR requires three or more of the following behaviors to occur within twelve months for the diagnosis of substance dependence:

- tolerance
- withdrawal
- individual uses the substance longer than they meant to
- uncontrollable desire

- spending a lot of time getting, using or recovering from substance
- individual gives up important things because of usage
- abuse continues even though the individual knows that it is bad.

For the diagnosis of substance abuse one or more of the following must happen within twelve months:

- individual does not fulfill responsibilities due to substance usage
- individual puts herself in danger while using substance
- legal problems related to substance usage
- continuing to use substance even though it is causing problems with others.

Agoraphobia

Individuals with a panic disorder experience panic attacks in which they feel an extreme increase in anxiety. Agoraphobia is the fear of places or situations that are hard to get away from like buses, open spaces, elevators or driving over bridges. A person can have agoraphobia with or without panic attacks. The DSM-IV-TR requires the following symptoms for a diagnosis of agoraphobia without panic disorder:

- the individual shows agoraphobic tendencies because they are afraid of vomiting or otherwise becoming physically ill
- the agoraphobia doesn't happen because of a medical problem or drug
- if the person does have a medical problem they are more afraid than normal.

For a diagnosis of panic disorder without agoraphobia a patient must have all of the signs of panic disorder with agoraphobia except the agoraphobia symptoms.

Agoraphobia with panic attacks

For a diagnosis of panic disorder with agoraphobia a patient must have a panic attack plus at least one of the following:

- always worrying about having more panic attacks
- being worried about what might happen if they do have another panic attack
- changes in behavior because of the panic attacks.

The patient must also have agoraphobia and the panic attacks can't be caused by other medical or psychological illness. This illness usually develops quickly without definite causes. Often the first diagnosis of panic disorder is in the emergency room after the patient having a panic attack will feel as if they are having a heart attack and/or are dying. Psychotherapy has the best rate of treatment and these patients usually do get better.

Anorexia nervosa and bulimic nervosa

Two disorders related by exhibiting extreme behaviors in order to lose weight, unnatural fear of becoming over eight and distorted body image are anorexia and bulimia nervosa. Both of these disorders are usually seen in teenage girls but they are beginning to be seen more often young girls and adolescent boys. In order to meet the DSM-IV-TR requirements for anorexia nervosa the individual must show the following behaviors:
- refusing to maintain a healthy weight
- not believing that their weight is unhealthy or they believe that they are fat
- no having three periods in a row.

The diagnosis of bulimia nervosa is characterized by eating a very large amount of food in a short time and feeling no self control. After binging bulimics perform acts that will keep them from gaining weight such as making themselves throw-up, taking too many laxatives, refusing to eat or exercising too much.

ADHD

Attention deficit hyperactivity disorder (ADHD) symptoms include the inability to concentrate and increased aggression. Stimulant medication is often used to good effect including Ritalin, Cylert and Dexedrine. The DSM-IV-TR lists three types of ADHD:
- ADHD Inattentive
- ADHD Hyperactive-Impulsive and
- ADHD combined.

For a diagnosis of ADHD inattentive the child must have six or more of the following lasting at least six months:
- does not pay attention in school

- short attention span
- doesn't pay attention to verbal commands
- doesn't finish assignments
- low organizational skills
- doesn't like to do things that require thinking
- loses important things
- easily distracted
- forgetful.

ADHD hyperactivity-impulsive requires six in six months of these:
- unable to keep still
- will not stay in seat
- runs and climbs in odd places
- unable to play quietly
- talks too much
- always "on the go"
- tries to answer a question before I has been completely asked
- doesn't want to wait
- interrupts the conversations of other people.

Autism

Diagnosis of autism according to the DSM-IV-TR is complex and requires six symptoms to be observed according to the rules of three separate lists. Two from list one:
- unable to use nonverbal communication
- unable to make friendships within own age range
- unable to share feelings with other people
- unable to reply in kind in social situations.

One from list two:
- not able to speak and does not try to communicate via non-speech means
- children who can speak are not able to have conversations

- uses the same word or phrase over and over or uses unusual language
- does not imitate or play make-believe.

One from list three:
- has an unnatural fixation in one area of interest
- repeats the same action over and over
- repeats the same movements over and over
- focuses on parts rather than the whole;

as well as at least one of these symptoms occurring before age three:
- problems with social behaviors
- problems with social speech
- lack of make-believe play.

Bipolar disorder

People who have bipolar disorder have times when they are very happy and over-animated, mania, and times when they are very unhappy, depression. The DSM-IV-TR lists four types of bipolar disorder seasonal affective disorder, cyclothymia, Bipolar I and Bipolar II. Lithium is the most prescribed drug for this disorder but Depakote, Tegretol and Lamictal are also used.

Individuals with seasonal affective disorder (SAD) show changes in their mood according to the changing seasons. Usually they are maniac in spring and summer and depressed in the fall and winter. Phototherapy used during the depressed state can be very helpful. Cyclothymia involves dysthymia, moderate chronic depression, broken by times of hypomania. This diagnosis can be made for children and adolescents after one year of symptoms and after two years for adults. In order to be diagnosed as Bipolar I an individual only needs to have had one manic episode. These individuals do not have symptoms for full depression though they may through stages of mixed behavior. Bipolar II is marked by hypomania and major depression. People with Bipolar II disorder do not have times of mania or mixed behaviors.

BPD

People with borderline personality disorder (BPD) have problems with relationships and mood stability. They may see things as either all bad or all good. Dialectical behavior therapy and selective serotonin reuptake inhibitors are sometimes used in the treatment process, however the treatment outlook is not particularly positive for this disorder. The DSM-IV-TR states that BPD must have an onset in early adulthood. To receive a diagnosis of BPD an individual most show at least five of the following symptoms:

- intense efforts to avoid being left
- patter of seeing other people as either all good or all bad
- confused self-image
- impulsive behavior or
- self mutilation
- unstable mood
- feeling empty
- outbursts of anger
- paranoid thinking brought on by stress.

Clinical depression

Clinical depression manifests itself in four areas of functioning:

- physical (feeling tired),
- behavioral (unable to complete tasks),
- cognitive (feelings of unworthiness), and
- emotional (extreme sadness).

Individual have a five to ten percent chance that they will get clinically depressed in their lifetime. People who are more likely to become depressed are women, the elderly, the poor and those with a family history of depression. There are several therapy ideas for depression including psychoanalysis, cognitive therapy, behavioral therapy and medications such as monoamine oxidase inhibitors and tricyclics. The three most popular drugs currently are fluoxetine, citalopram, and bupriopion. Dysthymia is a type of depression marked by long term feelings of sadness.

DSM-IV-TR

According to the DSM-IV-TR a patient must show five or more of the following problems in a two week time span in order to be diagnosed with major depression:

- inability to be happy, feeling very sad or uninterested normal activities

- feeling sad almost all day every day
- loss of interest or inability to be happy almost all day every day
- extreme weight gain or weight loss, or wanting to eat more or less than usual
- sleeping too much or not being able to sleep
- feeling tired
- feeling unwarranted guilt or low self-esteem
- unable to think or concentrate properly
- thoughts or actions or plans of suicide.

Conduct disorder

Conduct disorder is seen in children and adolescents as extreme aggression (both physically and verbally), disobedience and destructiveness. Family therapy is often employed in the treatment of this disorder as environmental factors play a large role in the causation of the disorder. Some children may first have oppositional defiant disorder. The DSM-IV-TR requires that at least four of the following be displayed within six months:
- temper tantrums
- argumentative
- uncooperative
- displays purposeful annoying behavior
- unwilling to accept blame
- easily annoyed
- angers easily
- wishes to "get even".

A diagnosis of conduct disorder is made when three or more of the following behaviors occur within one year:
- is a bully
- picks fights
- uses weapons
- physically hurts people or animals
- commits violent theft
- rapes or otherwise forces sexual activity
- sets fires in order to cause damage

- destroys property
- engages in breaking and entering
- lies frequently
- commits shoplifting or other non-violent theft
- stays out late at a young age
- runs away from home
- plays hooky from school.

DO and Asperger's disorder

Developmental disabilities (DD) begin in childhood and last until death. DD are very severe problems either mental or physical or both. Pervasive developmental disorders are the term used for DD by the American Psychiatric Association. The Denver Developmental Screening Test is used to assess children for DD. Three such disorders are Asperger's, Rhett's and childhood disintegrative disorder.

A diagnosis of Asperger's disorder according to the DSM-IV-TR requires a minimum of two of these:
- inability to use nonverbal action correctly
- unable to make friends in same age group
- does not actively share joy
- unable to behave appropriately in social situations.

Children must also have at least one of the following symptoms:
- intense focus on one item of interest
- unable to stop doing the same thing over and over
- performing the same movements over and over
- seeing parts as more interesting than the whole.

Disintegrative disorder and Rhett's disorder

Children who seem normal until the age of two but then seem to regress may have childhood disintegrative disorder. The DSM-IV-TR requires the child to regress in at least two of the following:

- communication
- social skills
- toileting habits
- play
- motor development.

They must also display two of the following:
- measurable changes for the worse in the ability to make friends communicate, understand non-verbal cues, or social skills
- measurable worsening of the ability to speak or understand spoken language, using odd language, imaginative play
- performing the same actions over and over.

Rhett's disorder begins after five months of age with the child seeming normal until then. Afterwards they must display all of the following:
- head grows at a slower than normal rate
- unable to use hands at will
- unable to engage socially
- inefficient walking
- extreme retardation of communication skills.

Acute and post-traumatic stress disorders

According to the American Psychiatric Association there are two related stress disorders known as acute and post traumatic. The primary difference of these two disorders is that acute stress disorder lasts for four weeks or less while post-traumatic stress disorder (PTSD) has no time limit. Both disorders are developed in association with witnessing or being a victim of disaster, including plane crashes, earthquakes and war. Individuals may have flashbacks or nightmares were they relive the trauma over and over. They may also try to stay away from people or places that bring to mind the trauma. For example, a veteran of a foreign war may no longer associate with his army pals. Also they have a general increase in anxiety.

Gender-identity disorder

Gender-identity disorder is defined as the strong desire or belief that one is of the opposite gender. Boys may hope that their penis will fall off while girls wish to grow one. When this disorder continues into adulthood it leads to the desire to have sex reassignment surgery, known as transsexualism. It happens to men more than women. The DSM-IV-TR asks that the following conditions be met for a diagnosis of gender-identity disorder. At least four of these symptoms:

- says many times that he/she is of the opposite sex
- boys will enjoy wearing dresses while girls refuse to wear dresses or skirts
- pretends to be other sex in games or daydreams
- extreme wish to play sports or games usually associated with the opposite sex
- only want to be friends with members of the opposite sex.
- Boys have a sense that their penis is gross.
- Girls refuse to sit while urinating and desire not to develop breasts.

Personality disorders

Personality disorders are often marked by a need for attention. They are the cause for improper behavior in relationships and social situations. Symptoms of personality disorders are usually found to be affecting the way a person thinks, how they cope with emotions, the types of relationships they have, and their ability to control impulses.

The DSM-IV-TR requires that five of the following behaviors be established by early adulthood in order to receive a diagnosis of histrionic personality disorder:

- needs to be the center of attention in order to feel comfortable
- often uses sexual come-ons in improper situations
- emotions change quickly and are never very deep
- tries to gain attention with how they look
- speaks using a false voice
- over exaggeration of emotions (diva behavior)
- depends on others for beliefs
- sees friendships as being more affectionate than they truly are.

OCD

Obsessive-compulsive disorder (OCD) is a type of anxiety disorder in which individuals are unable to control stressful thought (obsession) and feel the urge to do the same behaviors repeatedly (compulsion) in an effort to relieve stress. Behavioral therapy has been shown to have very high rates of success. In habituation the patient is exposed to the stressor but not aloud to act on the compulsion, after a time of extreme stress the patient becomes used to the stressor so that it no longer produces stress. Sometimes antidepressants such as clomipramine are used in the treatment of OCD. The DSM-IV-TR defines obsessions as having the following characteristics:

- ideas which occur repeatedly for long periods of time and cause stress
- ideas are not about real problems
- patient tries to keep from thinking about stressful ideas
- patient realizes that the ideas are created from within.

Compulsions have the following characteristics:

- physical or mental behaviors which are repeated with strict rules governing there methods
- physical or mental behaviors that the patient uses to relieve stress even though the behaviors are not realistically important.

Somatoform disorders

Somatoform disorders all share in common the symptom of psychological pain manifesting itself as physical pain or defect. Also it is important to remember that medically speaking nothing is wrong with these patients.

Conversion disorders

Conversion disorders happen when a person feels guilty over the urge to commit some unacceptable behavior. So that the act becomes physically impossible the person's mind converts the thought into a disability. For example a man has an extreme urge to watch his neighbor undress even though he knows it is morally wrong. After fighting this urge for sometime he goes blind and the urge is gone.

Hypochondriasis

Hypochondriasis is the fear or belief that one is terribly ill. Often the person can think of little else besides the presumed illness to the point that the person's social life is affected.

Somatization and pain disorders

Individuals with somatization and pain disorders complain of symptoms from many different illnesses and truly believe that the symptoms are real. For a diagnosis of somatization the DSM-IV-TR requires that the disorder being before age thirty and display all of the following characteristics:

- patient complains of pain in at least four different parts of the body
- a minimum of two complaints of stomach problems other than pain
- at least one complaint of sexual problems other than pain
- at least one neurological complaint.

The individual must also show one of the following:

- after having been seen and checked out by a doctor the complaints has no basis in reality
- if the person really does have a medical problem related to the complaints the problems are much worse than normal.

For a diagnosis of pain disorder the DSM-IV-TR requires that the perceived pain is in more than one location and the pain results in a lower ability to function. The pain must also have been triggered by something psychological.

Impulse control disorders

Individuals with impulse control disorders have uncontrollable urges to behave impulsively and receive and emotional thrill from doing so. These behaviors are not addictions which are classified separately.

Intermittent explosive disorder

The DSM-IV-TR defines intermittent explosive disorder behaviors as acts which cause personal or property damage. In order to be diagnosed with intermittent explosive disorder the patient must have behaved in the above manner several times with little or no provocation.

Pathological gambling

A diagnosis for pathological gambling requires that five of the following symptoms occur:
- constantly thinking about gambling
- obtaining happiness requires gambling more and more money
- the individual tries to stop numerous times
- withdrawal behaviors when trying to quit
- gambling is used as an escape mechanism
- tries to win back previous loses
- lies about gambling
- commits illegal act to get more money to gamble
- placing gambling ahead of important relationships
- expects other people to give them money.

Kleptomania

Kleptomania, pyromania and trichotillomania are all similar in that they give the individual a release from stress. Kleptomania is the uncontrollable urge to steal things. Before stealing these individuals become stressed which transforms into feelings of relief and happiness during the act. Stealing is done for the fun of it rather than for personal gain or because of anger.

Pyromania

People with pyromania purposely light fires out of curiosity. They are also drawn to things connected to fires such as matches, burned buildings or fire fighters. Often they stay on the sight of the fire in order to be an "eye-witness" which gives them the thrill of notoriety without being caught.

Trichotillomania

Trichotillomania is a condition in which a person receives stress relief from pulling out their hair. Sometimes they may even eat the pulled hair. Often they are left with bald patches on their scalps.

Expressive language disorder

Language is spoken or written symbols which allow people to exchange ideas. Language is made up of four parts: phonemes are the individual sounds; semantics are those sounds which have meaning, for example in the word cats there are two sounds with meaning, cat and s; grammar is the rules by which words and sentences are made; pragmatics are the social rules of language, where and when certain types of speech are aloud. The DSM-IV-TR defines expressive language disorder as a collection of symptoms which include:

- small vocabulary
- confusion with tense
- problems remembering specific words
- problems performing language skills at grade level.

In addition to these symptoms individuals with mixed receptive-expressive language disorder have problems understanding the meaning of language.

Learning disorders

Learning disorders are usually noticed in young children. The following are required for a diagnosis of a learning disorder:

- school work is below the guideline level for their age
- the disability creates problems for the child in daily life
- if the child has a medical condition affecting one of the sense the learning problems are worse than normal.

The DSM-IV-TR gives four types of learning disorders on Axis I: reading disorder; mathematics disorder; disorder of written expression; learning disorder not otherwise specified. Approximately five percent of school age children can be classified as learning disabled with an equal amount of girls and boys. It is believed that a combination of genetics and neurophysiologic factors lead to problems in the child's ability to think which in turn leads to learning disabilities. Identification of children with a learning disorder is very important as environmental changes to their educational set-up can vastly improve their prognosis.

TCAs

Tricyclic antidepressants (TCAs) work to suppress the action of neurotransmitters in the brain. Patients using TCAs usually see a change in their symptoms in two to four weeks. Side effects include feeling sleepy, light headedness, constipation, problems with vision and dry mouth. The following are the most common TCAs with their generic and trade name: amitriptyline, Elavil; amoxapine, Asendin; clomipramine, Anafranil; desipramine, Norpramin; doxepin, Sinequan, Adapin; imipramine, Toframil, Aventil; nortriptyline, Pamelor; protriptyline, Vivactil; trimipramine, Surmontil. Miscellaneous drugs that were not originally created for use in clinical depression but have come to be used in that area are: bupropion, Wellbutrin; mirtazapine, Remon; nefazodone, Serzone; trazodone, Desyrel; venlafaxine, Effexor.

SSRIs

Selective serotonin reuptake inhibitors (SSRIs) are now the number one category of drugs used in the treatment of clinical depression. These drugs are popular because they do not cause dizziness or light headedness. Some common side effects are feeling sick to the stomach, headache, and sexual malfunction. The following are the most common SSRIs listed with their generic and trade name: citalopram, Celexa; escitalopram oxalate, Lexapro; fluoextine, Prozac, Sarafem; fluvoxamine, Luvox; paroxetine, Paxil; sertraline, Zoloft. Monoamine oxidase inhibitors (MAOIs) are usually held only for the most serious cases of depression when nothing else tried as worked. Side effects include increase in weight, sexual malfunction, lowered blood pressure and thyroid dysfunction. The following are the most common MAOIs listed with their generic and trade name: phenelzine, Nardil; tranylcypromine, Parnate.

Sleep disorders and dementia

Sleep disorders are commonly caused by the natural drop in melatonin as a person ages. Medications used for sleep disorder help the individual fall asleep faster and stay asleep longer. In the past doctors were hesitant to prescribe medications for sleep disorders because most were habit forming however new drugs have recently come onto the market that are not. The following are the most common medications used for sleep disorders listed with their generic and trade name: donzepril, Aricept; tacrine, Cognex; zolpidem, Ambien. Three drugs typically used for sleep disorders are also used for dementia. They are donzepril, tacrine and zolpidem. The most common side effect for these drugs is sleepiness. Other drugs used in the treatment of dementia are listed here with their generic and trade name: estazolam, ProSom; flurazepam, Dalmane; quazepam, Doral; temazepam, Restoril; triazolam, Halcion.

Anxiety disorders

There are many types of anxiety disorders but most involve extreme fear of something or a situation also known as a phobia. Some common anxiety disorders are agoraphobia, kleptomania and addictive personality. It is not completely known what causes anxiety disorders; however risk factors include genetics, being a victim of violence, and low self-esteem. These disorders can often have a negative effect on how a person behaves even during important event, work driving, etc. The person finds it nearly impossible to stop worrying and does so a majority of the time. In order to be diagnosed with a generalized anxiety disorder the adult must have three (children need only show one) of the following behaviors:

- feeling hyped up
- getting tired easily
- problems with concentration
- easily angered
- inability to relax
- sleep problems.

Mental retardation

Anyone with an IQ lower than 70 falls into the definition of mentally retarded. However, there are four categories of mental retardation based on IQ mild, IQ 70-50; moderate, IQ 50-35; severe, IQ 35-20; and profound, IQ less than 20. Another way to classify individuals with this problem is by the amount of help they need in daily life; these four classes are:

- intermittent, only needs occasional help
- limited, needs help regularly with certain tasks
- extensive, can not live alone are completely take care of self
- pervasive, is unable to do anything without help.

There are many reasons why a person may be mentally retarded including genetics and fetal exposure to harmful substances. Some other causes are cerebral palsy, brain malformations or injuries and infectious disease.

There are over 1000 genetic factors that can be implicated in mental retardation. Perhaps the most well known is Down syndrome which is defined as trisomy 21. A genetic disorder which is inherited and causes mental retardation is the fragile X syndrome, however not all individuals with this syndrome have below average intelligence. Phenylketonuria (PKU) is a genetic disorder affecting the individual's ability to metabolize amino acids. If left untreated it can lead to mental retardation. Environmental causes of mental retardation that are known to affect the fetus are: diabetes, if uncontrolled in the mother, radiation exposure, and malnutrition during pregnancy. The largest environmental cause is alcohol. When infants are born of mothers who drank during pregnancy they are diagnosed with fetal alcohol syndrome. Fetal alcohol syndrome is also one of the preventable causes of mental retardation as the consumption of alcohol is completely under the mother's control.

Multiple personality disorder

Multiple personality disorder is a mechanism that abused children use to help them deal with the abuse while maintaining a façade of normality. Some individuals have one or more completely separate alternate personalities, one of which has absolutely no memory of the abuse. In other cases the main personality may remember the abuse but disassociates from the emotional aspects of it leaving that for another personality. One of the main problems with diagnosing and treating disassociative identity disorder (DID), the new term designated by the American Psychiatric Association for multiple personality disorder, is that the disorder is completely in the mind of the patient. Treatment for DID is a long and mentally painful process. The patient must talk about the abuse which originally brought about the disorder. The first thing that must happen when therapy beings is to stop any self-injurious behaviors. The second objective is to recognize each alternate personality and take care of their individual problems. The ultimate objective is to bring the separate alternate personalities back into one whole.

Paranoia

Paranoia is the condition in which an individual has a false understanding of the world or sees or hears things that are not there (delusions). While paranoia is used by most people the term delusional disorder is used by psychologists. Delusional disorder usually begins in middle adulthood. There are no known causes for this disorder and treatment outlook is very poor. In order to be diagnosed with delusional disorder the DSM-IV-TR states that the patient must have delusions of things that could actually be true. Behavior that is not part of the delusion should be normal. There are seven categories of paranoia base on the content of the delusions:

- Erotomanic, belief that someone loves them
- Grandiose, belief that they are extremely special in some way
- Jealous, belief that their mate is cheating
- Persecutory, belief that someone is trying to hurt them
- Somatic, belief that they are ill
- Mixed
- Unspecified.

Paranoid personality disorder

Paranoid personality disorder is related to delusional disorder. This problem is marked by the belief that many people are trying to do him harm in all aspects of their life. The most effective treatment is a mixture of drugs and cognitive therapy. The DSM-IV-TR requires at least four of the following symptoms be observed in order for a diagnosis to be made:

- believes, without any proof, that people are lying, misusing or hurting him
- constantly thinks about the allegiance of others

- does not want to tell important information about his life for fear it will be used against him
- mistakes everyday comments for ill wishes
- unwilling to forgive
- thinks people are attacking his reputation
- believes mate is cheating on him.

Phobias

Phobia is defined as an extreme fear of something harmless or neutral. The fear has no basis in reality. There are two main categories of phobias specific and social. Specific phobias are fears toward everyday objects such as dogs, bridges, or heights. When an individual is presented with the phobia they have an anxiety attack so they often go out of their way to avoid them. Even though they know that their fear isn't based in reality they have no control over it and only rarely try to get help for the problem. In social phobia an individual is afraid of looking bad in front of other people. They often become anxious simply thinking about certain social situations and take extreme measures to avoid having to meet new people or attending a large gathering. Typically they are afraid of social situation in general rather than one specific type.

RAD

Children who are raised in an institutional setting or in a neglectful situation often show a number developmental disabilities. Reactive attachment disorder (RAD) has only recently been added to the list of developmental disorders recognized by the American Psychiatric Association. RAD has an age of onset of less than five years. For a diagnosis of RAD to be made the child must be in a setting were at least one of the following is true:
- child's emotional needs are not met
- child's physical needs are not met
- child often moves from one caregiver to another.

Children who are removed from the poor environment at a young age are likely to make a full recovery. RAD can be diagnosed by observing either inhibited or disinhibited behaviors. Inhabited behaviors are the inability to act appropriately in social situations and difficulty forming relationships with caregivers. Disinhibited behaviors are marked by the child

- 56 -

forming tenuous attachments to people that are unimportant in their lives.

Schizophrenia

One of the most severe mental disorders, schizophrenia affects all aspects of a person's life due to its problem set. There are four subtypes of schizophrenia.
- Catatonic schizophrenia is defined by abnormal body movements.
- Disorganized schizophrenia is characterized by little or improper emotions and the inability to understand; these patients may also exhibit signs of catatonic schizophrenia.
- Paranoid schizophrenia is characterized by the patient constantly thinking about or "living in" a false reality.
- The fourth subtype known as undifferentiated schizophrenia is used when the patient's problems do not neatly fit into one of the other three types.

The DSM-IV-TR requires a minimum of two of the following symptoms for a diagnosis of schizophrenia:
- a system of false beliefs
- seeing or hearing things that are not real
- unable to speak properly
- abnormal body movements
- little to no emotion.

Separation anxiety

Nearly all children go through a normal period of separation anxiety. Problems occur when the anxiety does not resolve on its own or becomes so extreme that it interferes with day to day functioning. A mixture of cognitive and behavior therapies lead to the best results in treating this disorder. The DSM-IV-TR requires at least three of the following behaviors to continue for a minimum of four weeks for a diagnosis of separation anxiety:
- becoming extremely upset when leaving or thinking about leaving the focus of their attachment
- constantly being concerned that something bad will happen to their loved one
- constantly being concerned that something bad will happen to take them away from the focus of their attachment

- constantly refuses to leave because is afraid to be without attachment figure
- afraid of being alone
- constantly refuses to go to sleep without loved one nearby
- bad dreams
- shows signs of psychosomatic illness when leaving or thinking about leaving the source of attachment.

Paraphilias

Sexual behaviors which fall outside of societal norms and are problematic for the individual or illegal are known as paraphilia. The DSM-IV-TR requires the behaviors to last at least six months, happen over an over and be so strong as to keep the person from normal sexual intercourse. Exhibitionism is showing a stranger one's genitals in a public place. Fetishism is characterized by the use of inanimate objects. Frotteurism takes place when a person purposely touches or rubs someone else without their knowledge or consent, usually done with clothing on. Pedophilia is the desire to be intimate with children under the age of thirteen. Sexual masochism is defined as the need to be physically or mentally harmed for sexual stimulations. Sexual sadism is the desire to dominate. Transvestic fetishism is the use by men of women's clothing for sexual purposes. Voyeurism is watching someone undress or be naked without their knowledge or consent.

Proxemics

Proxemics is the study of personal/group space. Personal space is influenced by gender (males prefer more space than females), feelings (people who like one another need less space between them than those who dislike one another), and rank (people who are equally ranked require less space between them than people who are unequally ranked). Another aspect of proxemics is territoriality. Territoriality is the felling of ownership over an area of space. When an individual is on "home turf" he feels more comfortable. Generally, men show more territorial behaviors than women. Crowding is the third area of proxemic research. The number of people within a set space which equals crowding varies from individual to individual. If an individual is exposed to an uncomfortable amount of crowding long term he may become more aggressive or withdrawn, his blood pressure may rise and heart health may worsen, and his ability to function cognitively will probably be impaired. The last area of proxemics is privacy. Privacy is the need to be alone. This need is very different for every individual depending on the situation, personality, learned behaviors, and culture.

Effects of the environment on client behavior

There are three ways to look at the effects of the environment on an individual's behavior. The first focuses on how an individual takes in facts from her surroundings and how she files these facts in her brain. Research has shown that developmental stage influences the way an individual views and organizes the surroundings. The second focuses on how an individual feels about and appraises her surroundings. An individual's personality is a primary factor in how she expresses feelings about her surroundings. The third focuses on how an individual interacts with her surroundings. An individual with high self-esteem will react to the surroundings more positively and in more productive ways than an individual with low self esteem.

<u>Environmental theories of behavior</u>

There are four basic theories that are generally believed to effect an individual's interaction with her environment. The first theory, known as trait or formist, looks at the individual separately from their surroundings. This theory believes that the environment has no or little effect on the personality. When research is carried out using this theory the ways in which different personalities interact with their surroundings is the focus of study. Causal interaction between individuals and their surroundings is looked at in the interactional view. For example an elderly person avoids icy weather for fear of falling. The organismic view maintains that interaction between individual and her surroundings are very important and change one another. In other words personality is not formed only from within. Contextual theories do not attempt to separate the individual from the environment choosing to view them as a single functioning organism instead.

Abuse & neglect

Child Abuse Prevention and Treatment Act

The Child Abuse Prevention and Treatment Act defines child abuse and neglect as, "any recent act or failure to act on the part of a parent or care taker that results in death, serious physical or emotional harm, or sexual abuse or exploitation or an act or failure to act that presents an imminent risk of serious harm." This means that abuse may be active, hitting a child, or passive, allowing someone else to hit a child. Physical abuse of a child includes anything that results in the physical injury of the child. Parents for example may spank their children but if the spanking leaves bruises then it is abuse. Sexual abuse may take the form of committing sexual acts with a child, forcing the child to perform sexual acts with others or engaging the child in pornography. Sexual abuse is most often not reported because of the shame felt by the child or the child having been threatened with further violence by the abuser.

Child neglect and emotional abuse

Neglect of a child can take the forms of physical, educational or emotional. Physical neglect may be withholding medical care or forcing the child to leave the home. Leaving the child alone is also a form of neglect, however the line at which neglect begins depends on the physical age of the child, the developmental age of the child and the community definition of inadequate supervision. Sufferers of this form of neglect, sometimes known as "latch key children" are growing in number due to the increase in single parent households as well as the increase in dual income households. Emotional abuse towards children often goes undetected as it leaves no outward signs and can be difficult to prove even with the child's testimony. Emotional abuse may include calling the child hurtful names, blaming the child for problems in which the child has no control, or extreme punishments. An example of extreme punishment is forcing the child to sit in a dark closet for long periods of time.

Factors involved in child abuse

Within the United States there are approximately one million cases of child abuse per year. Most likely this number is smaller than the actual reality due to the underreporting of abuse. African American children have the highest incidence of abuse while Asian Americans have the lowest. Girls are far more likely to experience sexual abuse than boys. Adolescents and children under the age of five of both sexes are most likely to be seriously injured due to physical abuse. Due most likely to socio-economic factors children who are born prematurely or of low birth weight suffer abuse more than others. Also children who are mentally or physically handicapped are at far greater risk. The majority of child abuse is perpetrated by women. However, men more commonly physically injure children during abusive behavior and have the highest incidence of sexual abusive behaviors towards girls and boys. High stress levels and low tolerance toward frustration are two factors involved in the personality of people who abuse children. Also a higher percentage of abusive parents are unemployed and/or poorly educated than those that don't abuse.

Consequences of abuse

The effect of abuse on children involves several factors. The extent of abuse can change outcome scenarios for children who have been abused. Also the child's developmental stage at the time of the abuse can markedly affect a child's chance of surviving "intact" given the same type and level of abuse. Children who are abused must learn to cope with the situation in whatever way the can. Miss-learned coping mechanisms as well as suppression can lead to psychological problems in general and specifically to personality disorders. Some personality disorders commonly associated with a possible history of child abuse include borderline personality disorder and dissacociative (split personality) disorder.

Signs of child abuse

Signs that a child is being abused can be observed in all stages of development. Infants may fail to gain weight or even loose weight, they may fail to reach social and developmental milestones or be particularly fretful. Toddlers and preschoolers may be withdrawn, unable or unwilling to play with peers, unable to engage in imaginative play or overaggressive, imitating the abuse they receive. If a child of this age is sexually precocious it is almost a definite sign of sexual abuse. School-aged children and adolescents are likely to have low self-esteems, have problems socializing in developmentally correct ways, and become depressed or violent. Often these children are mislabeled as social deviants and do not get the help the need and deserve.

Why child abuse occurs

The most recognized theory of why child abuse occurs is based on the ecological model. The ecological model explains abuse as a multifaceted problem. Often there are outside pressures and the society as a whole does not completely condemn child abuse.

Some children appear to do ok despite having been abused. Research into their personalities may lead to new theories and treatments in the field of psychology. Prevention of abuse is a large focus of individuals who work with adults and children. Sometimes the parent needs only a proper education in the correct way to raise a child. Free or reduced cost counseling for parents can also reduce the risk of them becoming abusers. Finally it must be recognized that until children are free from the pressures of homelessness, poverty and inadequate health care child abuse will continue.

Indicators of danger to self and others

Adolescents

There are three stages ranked by the proximity to a dangerous event occurring at the hands of an adolescent. The first behaviors that should be taken as a warning that an adolescent may become a danger to himself or others are:

- feeling left out
- removing himself from social activities
- feeling that no one wants him
- becoming a victim of aggression
- feeling like people are trying to harm him mentally
- worsening grades and wanting to go to school
- writing about or drawing violent images
- inability to control anger
- problems in the past with authority
- problems in the past with violence.

Intermediate behaviors are as follows:

- becoming or espousing racist ideology
- begins to use illegal substances
- joins or hangs out with a gang
- a way to get guns
- talking about or making threats of aggression.

Some imminent warning behaviors are:

- getting into fights
- destroying property
- gets very angry very easily
- serious threats of extreme aggression
- having a gun
- cutting or otherwise harming himself
- threatening suicide.

Young adults

The belief that if someone threatens or talks about suicide they would never go through with it is simply a myth. In fact talking about a wish to die is a sign that she will hurt herself. Sometimes a young adult may ask a family member or mentor for help. If this occurs do not take it lightly even if you don't believe she is capable of violence. Failing grades, if she is still at school, or trouble at work are also warning clues. Some observable changes include poor hygiene, not taking care of how she looks, little or no emotional response or extreme swings in emotions. Last is if she begins to show signs of drug or alcohol abuse.

Domestic violence

While domestic violence has no one set definition it can be thought of as harm done to an individual by a family member or intimate relation. Women are particularly prone to domestic violence. Forms of domestic violence are many and varied. Economic abuse takes place when an individual is not allowed money or the means to earn money even though she should be able to by law. Physical abuse is perhaps the most used way in which men try to restrict the actions of women. Often times a woman who is physically abused is made to feel that it is "all her fault" or that she "deserves" the abuse through the use of emotional abuse. One example of emotional abuse is to keep the individual from speaking to family members or making friends. Another example is when the abuser threatens to kill the abused individual or themselves. Since 1992 spousal rape has been illegal in the entire United States. Unfortunately though many people still do not recognize sexual abuse within the confines of marriage.

Family systems and feminist psychological theories of domestic violence

There are four primary theories as to the causes of domestic violence towards a wife at the hands of her husband. Family systems theory is based on the idea that both husband and wife have problems with self-esteem even before marriage. The husband may feel the need for domination over his wife because he fears close relationships, doesn't understand healthy dependent behavior, and an innate desire for control. In turn the woman may stay because she was abused or witnessed abuse as a child, doesn't have the proper coping skills or understand healthy dependent behavior. Lenore Walker developed the feminist psychological theory. This theory places a large part of the blame on society due to its negative effects on women through learned gender roles, sexism and the fact that women do not have pay equity. Walker also describes what she calls the "battered woman syndrome" as the reason why abused women stay and compares it with post-traumatic stress disorder.

Psychoanalytic theories of domestic violence

The learning theory of abuse combines ideas from social learning theory and cognitive behavioral therapy. This theory posits that they cycle of abuse is rooted in childhood experience. Children typically see men as being in charge or "the boss" in a variety of settings both inside and outside the family unit. Also children are far more likely to witness in person or on television and movies violence towards women by men than towards men by women. Even magazine ads prominently feature women in positions of submission. These ideas become part of the child's personality and lead to abusive/submissive behaviors as adults. The psychoanalytic theory is also based in childhood experience. In this case however the belief is that children have been the direct victims of or witnesses to domestic violence. This theory states that girls who are abused go on to become women that are abused because it is what they know and are psychologically comfortable with. These women choose violent men and may even goad the man into violence. Men become aggressors because they have seen, as boys, the power of violence to achieve desired results.

Age, alcohol and childhood factors in domestic violence

There are six factors that make it more likely that a woman will be a victim of domestic violence. When based on percentage data an adolescent is far more likely to be in an abusive relationship than an adult. This may be because individuals with abusive tendencies are more precocious than their peers. Approximately 25 percent of abuse takes place under the influence of alcohol. The exact number of alcoholics that participate in abuse is unknown. People who were not abused as children are less likely to become abusive adults than those who were. Boys who witness the abuse of a parent are three times more likely to grow up to abuse their wives than those who did not. Boys who witness extreme violence between their parents are 1,000 times more likely to become abusers.

Economic, race, and marital factors in domestic violence

Two factors of abuse that are highly related are race and economics. Families that are struggling financially are more likely to fall into a cycle of domestic violence. The stress of money problems often puts added strain on an already shaky relationship. Because minorities are more likely to live at or below the poverty line than Caucasians they are also more prone to domestic violence than Caucasians. Black women are 400 percent more likely to be abused then white women and 200 percent more likely to be abused than women of other minorities. Latina women are twice as likely to be victims of domestic violence as white women. Marriage also has an effect on the rate of domestic violence. Couples who are living together without being legally marriage are twice as likely to have an abusive relationship as couples that are legally married. The exact reasons for this are unknown but may include social isolation and lack of a clear commitment to the relationship.

Treatment of domestic violence according to feminist psychology and learning theory

Feminist psychological theory includes three levels of prevention management and treatment of domestic violence. First, social views on how men and women should behave must be changed. Second, women should be encouraged and educated to be in control over their own lives in order to prevent or stop abuse. Third, women who have been severally abused should be taken into shelters so that they can be physically removed from the situation until they can become mentally healthy again. Learning theory allows for marital and group counseling in the realm of domestic violence. Individuals must understand where and how they originally learned the dysfunctional behavior. Afterwards the individuals should be educated in the proper behaviors and given a chance to learn these behaviors via a system of trial and reward.

Treatment of domestic violence according to family systems and psychoanalytic theories

The family systems theory requires both husband and wife to participate in therapy and work to change their underlying personality problems as well as learn to deal with one another more healthily. According to this theory the child is often blamed for the problem of domestic violence either consciously or unconsciously. The problems of childhood and adolescence can often be traced back to witnessing domestic violence. Long term individual counseling using a psychoanalytic perspective is the suggestion of psychoanalytic theory. The abuse woman should strive to understand why she is choosing the wrong men and how to stop doing it. It involves teaching the woman to think systematically and find reasons for her behavior from her childhood experiences.

General assessment issues

Use of assessment

The term assessment is generally used when the counselor evaluates a client in person.

Typically the first few sessions of treatment are set aside specifically for assessment so that the counselor may learn about the client's main reason for seeking counseling as well as the factors in his life that relate to it. It is also important for the counselor and client to set goals together and to form a bond of trust. It is important that assessment take place face to face so that the counselor may also note the non-verbal clues given by the client in response to the environment and questions. Assessment may also include information learned about the client through standardized tests which the client does either in private or in the counselor's office. These tests may look at intelligence, personality, or preferences.

Specific assessments

Mental status exam

While not a formal psychological exam the mental status examination (MSE) can be very helpful in the process of assessment. The MSE contains six categories which the counselor can use to measure the client's overall state of well being. The first category regards how the client looks (appearance), how she reacts to the counselor (attitude) and her movements (activity). The client's feelings both inside (mood) and the formalization of them (affect) make up the second category. The third category concentrates on verbal abilities. Thoughts and the ability to think reasonably are looked at by the fourth and fifth categories. The final category takes into considerations the person's insight and judgment. This form of assessment is good because is includes information from the client and information observed by the counselor.

Personality tests

There are two ways to develop a personality test. The first, face validity has questions and answers that directly match to the trait that is being looked at and is theoretically based. For example a true-or-false question looking at self-esteem may read, "I don't like myself." The Beck Depression Inventory is an example of a face validity test. Empirical keying is another way to develop a psychological test. On this type of test the developer does not assign personality traits to the questions instead she has many hundreds of people complete the exam then compares the answers of "normal" people to the answers of people who have been diagnosed with a personality disorder. The questions and answers are studied to see which ones appear to indicate illness. The Minnesota Multiphasic Personality Inventory is one very popular empirically keyed test.

CPI and NEO-Personality Inventory

The California Psychological Inventory (CPI) is an empirically keyed exam consisting of 462 items that the subject answers "true" or "false" to. The items are broken down into twenty different personality categories. Furthermore the individual's personality is looked at according to the following three orders:

- outgoing versus solitary
- lives according to socially acceptable behavior versus does not
- overall happiness versus unhappiness.

The NEO-Personality Inventory (NEO-PI) was designed for and is used as an exam to study personality traits that do not exactly match disorders. These traits are commonly known as the "big five". They are extroversion, agreeableness, conscientiousness, neuroticism and open to experience.

TAT

The Thematic Appreciation Test (TAT) is a projective test which asks the test taker to tell a story about pictures that are shown to them. The pictures can be interpreted in many ways and the counselor asks the client to tell what happened before, after and during the moment depicted on the card. This test is usually administered one on one in order for the counselor to observe and write down the stories generated and to follow up with questions they might have, however the exam can be given in groups situations as long as they can read and write. The answers may be interpreted formally according to published guidelines or the exam may simply be used as an easy non threatening way to learn more information about the client.

MMPI

The Minnesota Multiphasic Personality Inventory (MMPI) was designed to help identify people with personality disorders, however it is also often used to profile "normal" personalities as well. On the MMPI-2 subjects are instructed to answer 567 items as "true" or "false". Within the exam are ten clinical categories and four validity scales. The clinical items are used to help diagnose disorders; while the validity items help to see whether the subject is telling the truth. The clinical measures are: hypochondriasis, depression, hysteria, psychopathic deviation, the degree to which a person relates to being male or female, paranoia, abnormal fear and obsessive compulsive disorder, schizophrenia, hypomania, introversion. The validity scales are:

- the "Cannot Say" scale, number of items not answered or marked both true and false
- the "L" scale, attempts to catch individuals that are trying to make themselves look different than is true
- the "F" scale, the scale measures the number of items marked opposite of 90 percent of other test takers
- the "K" scale tries to find individuals that are using defense mechanisms to change their scores.

Personality tests

There are five types of personality assessment used in social work: self report, projective tests, behavioral observation, interview, biological measures. Self-report measures usually take the form of questionnaires and inventories. An example is the Millon Clinical Multiaxial Inventory. Projective tests are open to interpretation be each counselor. Subjects are shown something can be seen differently by different people according to their personality and/or emotional state. The most famous example is the Rorschach inkblot test. Behavioral observations are assessments made by the counselor watching the client go about their daily tasks. This may be done in person, via video camera, or through phoning the patient throughout the day to ask what/how they are doing. Interviews can ask the same kind of questions as self-report but are done face to face. The counselor is able to consider both verbal and non-verbal responses. Biological measures can range from the simple, measuring breathing rates, to the advanced, looking at positron emission tomography (PET) scans.

PIAT

The Peabody Individual Achievement test (PIAT) was developed to measure the knowledge of school children from kindergarten to high school in six areas. The areas are:
- "General Information"
- "Reading Recognition"
- "Reading Comprehension"
- "Mathematics"
- "Spelling"
- "Written Expression".

Each area is administered differently including verbal question/verbal response, written text/verbal response, written text/picture choice. The PIAT can be given only to one individual at a time. The administrator begins with questions the child can answer easily and proceeds until the individual gets five out of seven wrong. The PIAT is generally used to make a specialized plan of education for the child but can also be used to see how program is going. A child's score is compared to the average score for children his age.

State-Trait Anxiety Inventory

The State-Trait Anxiety Inventory is the most popular anxiety self-report form. It is only twenty items long so is easily and quickly completed. The items are both positively and negatively termed and the individual chooses the answer (from "not at all" to "very much so") which best matches their feeling. This questionnaire has been formulated into different tests which can be used for children, care-givers, and people who speak other languages. The State-Trait Anxiety Inventory can be used for a variety of reasons. Perhaps the most common use is at the start of therapy and at measured times during and again after therapy is complete. Another use is before the start of medication for anxiety and again once the drug begins to take effect.

BDI and CDI

The Beck Depression Inventory (BDI) is a self-rating questionnaire developed in 1972. The BDI lists twenty-one common symptoms of depression and asks the individual to rate how they are feeling about each one on a scale of 0 for very little to 3 very much. Some of the symptoms measured include crying, not wanting to do things that used to be enjoyable, tiredness and lack of clear thinking. If the individual's score is more than thirty they may be very badly depressed. The Children's Depression Inventory (CDI) is a self-rating test for children aged seven to seventeen and based on the Beck Depression Inventory for adults. The child is asked to read a set of sentences and then tick the one that most represents the feelings they have had for two weeks. The child's score is compared with the scores of other children their age. This assessment has been translated into many languages and is used throughout the world.

Intervention planning

Benzodiazepine anxiolytics

Although many types of drugs can be used to treat anxiety benzodiazepine anxiolytics are prescribed the most often. One of the major side effects with this class of drugs is the possibility of addiction. Other side effects include sleepiness and light headedness. The following are the most common benzodiazepine anxiolytics listed with their generic and trade name: alprazolam, Xanax; buspirone, Buspar; chlordizapoxide, Librium; clorazepate, Tranxene; diazepam, Valium; hydroxyzine, Atarax, Vistrail, Marax; lorazepam, Ativan; oxazepam, Serax.

Mood stabilizing medications

Mood stabilizers used in the treatment of mania are actually drugs which prevent people from having convulsions but which have been found to be useful in this disorder. There are a number of serious side effects associated with these medications including lowered white cell count, sedation, rashes and tremors. There have been very few double-blind studies done with this class of drugs. Some mood stabilizers can poisonous so the dosages must be tightly controlled and blood levels monitored. The following are the most common mood stabilizers listed with their generic and trade name: carbamazepine, Tegretol; gabapentin, Neurontin; lamotrigine, Lamictal; lithium, Eskalith, Lithobid; valporic acid, Depakene, Depakote; verapamil, Calan, Isoptin, Verelan.

Neuroleptics

Neuroleptics are usually only used in very severe cases of mania or with patients that are in an institutional setting. These medications have all the usual side effects such as light headedness, vision problems and dry mouth. However, these medications all have some extremely serious side effects known as extrapyramidal symptoms (EPS). EPS includes a wide range of nervous systems disorders including shaking, tics, and body restlessness. Atypical neuroleptics have recently been approved for use with mania which does not show the same bad effects on the nervous system. The following are the most common neuroleptics listed with their generic and trade name: chlorpromazine, Thorazine; fluphenazine, Prolixin; haloperidol, Haldol; loxapine, Loxitane; mesoridazine, Serentil; perphenazine, Trilafon; pimozide, Orap; thioridazine, Mellaril; thiothixene, Navane; trifluoperazine, Stelazine. The following are the most common atypical neuroleptics listed with their generic and trade name: clozapine, Clozaril; olanzapine, Zyprexa; quetiapine, Seroquel; risperidone, Risperdal; ziprasidone, Geodon.

Stimulant medications

Stimulants are a class of drugs which lower the transmission of dopamine across the neural network. Stimulants make people feel happier and more awake. Minor side effects include body restlessness and irritability. Major side effects include the lowering of appetite which can lead to anorexia and growth suppression, lowering of thinking skills, and liver damage. The following are the most common stimulants listed with their generic and trade name: dextroamphetamine, Dexedrine, Dextrostat; dextroamphetamine saccharte/sulfate, amphetamine aspartate/sulfate, Adderal; methamphetamine hydrochloride, Desoxyn; methylphenidate, Ritalin, Metadate, Concerta, Methylin; modafinil, Provigil; pemoline, Cylert.

Direct and Indirect Practice

Primary prevention

Primary prevention on the community level seeks to develop and begin intervention programs before mental illness surfaces. Primary prevention has the effect of lowering both the raw number and percentage of people who become ill. The Women's Infants' and Children's (WIC) program is an excellent example of primary prevention at work. Through the WIC program pregnant women are given pre-natal nutrition counseling. Better pre-natal neutrino leads to healthier babies thus lowering the number of babies born with mental disabilities, the rate of child abuse and the number of physically disabled children. Other examples of primary prevention are sex education classes in high schools, vaccination programs and parenting classes.

Methods and Processes

Biofeedback mechanism

The human body carries on a number of processes throughout the day that the individual in never consciously aware of. When dealing with stress the body releases chemicals, raises respiration and blood pressure all without the individual ever noticing. Biofeedback therapy works by visibly showing the individual the results of stress on the body and teaching them to control these responses. Neal E. Miller believed that this control could be learned through instrumental conditioning and reinforcement. An application of biofeedback that can be successfully used by a social worker involves the galvanic skin response (GSR). A person's GSR can be used as an indication of stress. By using a GSR machine a person can learn to control the GSR and reduce stress.

Relaxation and rhythmic breathing

Two types of relaxation therapies used for stress intervention are progressive muscle relaxation and rhythmic breathing. Relaxation therapy can be used for a wide number of stress disorders as well as helping clients to learn proper coping techniques for a variety of situations. Edmund Jacobson developed progressive muscle relaxation. In this therapy individuals are asked to contract certain muscles for a count of five paying close attention to how the contraction feels before releasing them. Muscles are contracted together according to their group and all groups are contracted at some point during a session. After practice the client will be able to tell when he is contracting a muscle due to stress and in turn relax it. Rhythmic breathing is the process of breathing in through the nose and out through the mouth while silently counting. Breathing should be done deeply from the diaphragm in order to maximize its effectiveness. Meditation may be done in conjunction with rhythmic breathing in order to focus the individual on the breath alone.

Systematic rational restructuring

Systematic rational restructuring therapy is an extension of Albert Ellis's rational emotive therapy. Marvin Goldfried designed systematic rational restructuring therapy as a set of processes that the client must move through in order to rename or "restructure" their emotions. Goldfried believed that questionable behavior occurred because people incorrectly organize emotions during childhood. For example most people are not horribly terrified of spiders, but if a young child sees her mother react to a very large spider in an extreme way then the child might attach the emotion "extreme fear" to spiders in general. In therapy the client is told to think about the most minor circumstance that would cause anxiety. The client then lists irrational thinking tied to the circumstance, decide why they are irrational and to determine a rational response. This process is repeated many times with increasingly stressful scenarios. The client is also encouraged to test their irrational thinking in actual circumstances that cause them distress.

Stress inoculation

Stress inoculation is intended to work against anxiety and stress in the same way that vaccinations work against clinical disease. The client is first given small amounts of stress to cope with in order to get them used to it and to train them how to do it in the most competent way. There are three steps in stress inoculation training. In the first step, conceptualization, clients are asked to review their maladaptive thoughts and adopt more rational thinking strategies. With the second step, skill acquisition and rehearsal, the individual is educated in the behaviors that are better for handling occasions which cause them anxiety. The individual is also allowed to practice these new behaviors in a controlled environment so that they can become part of their nature. The final step is application and follow through. Clients are led through the first trials of application in the counselor's office which includes only very low levels of stress. Gradually the individual is given more difficult trials to work through at home. Once the individual is completely ready the engage in "follow through" by using the skills in real-life situations.

Self interest and social dilemmas

Self interest is a way of doing what is best only for the individual or specified group and is not generally favorable to cooperation with other individuals or groups. Unfortunately, in many cases what is best for an individual in the short term is hazardous to the community in the long term. This is especially the case in the consumption of resources. In order for a community to best use the limited resources available to them some level of cooperation is necessary. A community social worker must list the available resources, determine the community's short and long term goals, and find a way to distribute the resources that meet these goals.

Systematic desensitization intervention

While there are a number of behavioral techniques that can be used to help people with phobias systematic desensitization is perhaps the most popular due to its benign approach. Clients learn how to relax themselves at the start of each session in preparation for dealing with the phobia. At first the client merely thinks of the thing or situation that causes them distress. When thinking about it no longer causes anxiety they move onto the next level until eventually they confront the fear head on. For example if a person is afraid of spiders they begin by thinking of a drawing of a spider. When that can be done calmly they may look at actual photos of a spider, hold a fake spider, look at a real spider, touch the spider and finally hold the live spider without fear. This therapy is sued for a wide variety of phobias such as the fear of flying or the fear of heights.

Intervention techniques

Underage drinking interventions

College students are at high risk for drinking problems. Abstinence based courses do little to prevent students from beginning to drink or stopping students who are already over drinking. Brief intervention techniques, on the other hand, have been shown to be quite effective in reducing the number of alcohol related incidents among college students. Brief intervention helps students who are already drinking to think about how they are using alcohol in order to alter the amount they drink. For students who have not yet begun to drink brief intervention teaches them to drink in a responsible manner. Using the motivational interviewing model of counseling social workers accommodate all levels of predisposition to alter drinking practices. Motivational interviewing does not judge or confront the individual but tries to help them understand the problems that drinking is causing them. Another part of brief interventions uses skills training programs. These programs educate students to drink in a less hazardous manner. It is most persuasive when used together with motivational interviewing.

Intervention via flooding

Systematic desensitization uses calm step-by-step methods to help a client overcome fear, flooding on the other hand is done all at once using intense techniques. Flooding uses the body's mechanisms to train the client not to be afraid. The human body can sustain the emotion of fear for only a limited amount of time. Therefore flooding has the client start by thinking of their own "worst-case scenario". At first the client will probably feel very uncomfortable but after a time the body's autonomic responses will shut off and the client will be released from the state of fear. Flooding progresses far more quickly than systematic desensitization but the end results are the same and the two techniques have roughly the same percentage of cure rate. A related technique is known as imploding which adds psychodynamic qualities to the therapy.

Aversion therapy interventions

Aversion therapy is quite different to systematic desensitization and flooding which work to calm a client's fears because it attempts to make something the client enjoys become abhorrent. Aversion therapy is typically used with clients battling an addiction to food, cigarettes, or alcohol. An alcoholic may take the drug Anabuse which produces nausea after consuming alcohol. Aversion therapy can also be performed through thinking about a negative consequence. For example the overeater may think about eating their favorite food and then becoming horribly sick. Another method of aversion therapy uses a system of electric shock which occurs after the client sees cigarettes for example. There are several problems with this type of intervention. First using punishment is seen as a grey area ethically. Second long term effectiveness is seen only in a small portion of patients.

Behavioral intervention with children

The first step in the establishment of behavioral intervention is to define the questionable act and decide on the desired outcome of therapy. The desired outcome should be as specific as possible so that it can be monitored and evaluated. For example Sue, a five year old girl, refuses to give up her pacifier at bedtime. Her parents feel it is bad for her teeth but have let her continue because she cries and refuses to get in bed without it. In this case the problem behavior is Sue's use of the pacifier and acting up at bedtime. The desired outcome would state, "Sue will quietly go to bed and be able to sleep without her pacifier." The social worker next teaches the family or parents about the three principles of learning theory which are:

- recognize and stop reinforcing the questionable act
- reward good behavior that occurs in the place of the questionable behavior
- punishment should occur if the questionable behavior continues.

<u>Maintenance of behavioral intervention with children</u>

It is important to have the entire family involved with behavioral therapy including coming up with an individualized plan for treating the family member with the questionable behavior. The social worker should treat the parents as paraprofessionals once they have been educated in the principles of learning theory. For example for a boy who begins crying and screaming in the grocery store when his father won't buy his favorite cereal the plan may be to use a system of rewards and punishments. Following the stages of learning theory the father would tell his son before they leave for the grocery store that if he is good the whole time they can go for ice-cream afterwards. While shopping if the child looks ready to misbehave the father may give a small reminder such as saying, "ice-cream". This allows the child to choose good behavior. Finally if the questionable behavior continues once the other two steps have been implemented then punishment should be used. For example if the boy begins to scream for cereal even after being promised ice-cream and being gently reminded by his father, the father should pick up his son and take him home at once.

Brief therapy

Due to the rise in the cost of medical care and insurance a new type of therapy has been created known as brief therapy. As the name suggests brief therapy lasts for a short amount of time unlike traditional therapy which may go on for years. While there is no set number of sessions the maximum is typically twenty-five. At the first meeting between the social worker and client they decide exactly which problems will be addressed and how many sessions will be needed. Placing a time limit on problem resolution can be a fantastic source of motivation for some individuals. However, through the course of therapy other problems may be exposed which cannot be attended too because of the limited number of sessions. This therapy is generally recommended only for individuals who are overall mentally healthy and have only recently encountered a crisis situation.

Rational therapy

There are three well recognized types of rational therapies. Rational-emotive therapy is perhaps the best type of therapy which uses a cognitive behavioral approach. Albert Ellis developed rational-emotive therapy in the 1960's. The underlying principle is that individuals view the world from their own warped sense of reality which causes them unhappiness. It is the counselor's task to help the client understand and accept a more truthful view of reality.

Aaron T. Beck developed cognitive therapy to treat people suffering from depression. Beck believed that people who are depressed think bad things about themselves or their future. Cognitive therapy works by teaching the depressed person to think more positively.

Combining neuropsychology with a cognitive-behavioral approach, Maxie Maultsby advanced rational behavior therapy. Maultsby theorized that an individual's view of the surrounding environment brings about emotions which are either rational or irrational and behaviors follow. The counselor should lead the client in guided imagery helping them to focus on positive emotions and having the client perform proper behaviors.

Self control therapy and structural psychotherapy

Lynn Rehm combined the theories of behavior therapy and cognitive therapy to create self control therapy. Self control therapy works on the assumption that people who are depressed are more likely than non-depressed people to conduct the following tasks:
- pay more attention to adverse situations
- set personal goals higher than is possible to attain
- engage in far more self discipline than self accolades.

The client is taught how to better control their thoughts and behaviors so that they may overcome their depression. Structural psychotherapy is a complex set of ideas that encourages the client to step back from their dubious beliefs and attempt to view them as a disinterested scientist might. The therapy goes on to use the scientific method as a way for the client to determine which beliefs are rational and which are irrational. Structural psychotherapy is typically used with adults suffering from emotional disorders.

Self instructional therapy

Self-instructional therapy is a type of cognitive behavioral therapy used to treat children with impulse control problems. There are four steps in self-instructional therapy.
- The client watches the social worker do a simple activity, such as a put together a small puzzle, while giving herself instructions, like "take your time" or "stay focused".
- The child does the same task while the social worker gives him the same helpful reminders.
- The client does the task while reminding himself audibly.
- Eventually, the child practices the task with only internal reinforcement.

Self-instructional therapy can help children with impulse control problems on a variety of tasks and once the child has been properly trained he can transfer what he has learned from one task to another.

Music and arts therapies

Dance therapy

Dance therapy can be helpful for many types of mental illnesses in a variety of ways. People suffering from depression may find joy in the rhythmic body movements, sharing something with other people and stimulating music. Children who have problems with impulse control learn how to make their bodies perform in a desired fashion. Even aged and physically disabled patients can be helped through dance therapy. Through dance nonverbal individuals may be able to express deep emotion. Dance therapy can also be used as exercise for people with limited mobility. Dance therapy is generally approached in one of the following ways: humanistic, holistic health model, and the medical model.

Music therapy

Music therapy involves several of the body's senses to help a person manage their emotions, relate to other people, and relieve stress and anxiety. Music therapy involves listening to music, playing different types of musical instruments, and writing songs. All of these therapeutic actions may take place individually or in a group setting. Social workers can use elements of music therapy as part of an overall treatment plan, invite a certified music therapist to work within the group setting occasionally or refer clients to music therapists. Modern music therapy got its start after health care professionals noticed how well hospitalized veterans of World War II responded after attending small concerts within the hospital. No one kind of music best for music therapy. A client's tastes, treatment goals, and the counselor's knowledge of certain musical styles all have a place in deciding which music is used.

Art therapy

Art therapy uses the production of art to assess and treat people of all ages. Art therapy can easily be used in group settings and with families. Allowing the client to express their thoughts and feelings through art helps them to reduce stress, heighten their awareness of their body, and raise self-esteem. Art therapy is particularly useful when clients are dealing with a problem that it too difficult for them to discuss verbally. Sometimes children are first referred to a counselor after their teacher views something disturbing in their artwork. A social worker may attend continuing education workshops in order to learn how to apply art therapy in their own practice, invite a certified art therapist in for certain group or family sessions, or refer clients to an art therapist to see separately from the social worker.

Observational learning and modeling therapy

The idea of learning through watching is the basis for the observational learning and modeling theory. Children learn many things by watching the world around them. Adults too can learn technical skills by observation far more quickly than from simply reading about them. The individual performing (model) for the observer may be doing so live and in person or through pre-recorded images (film, televisions, etc.). For observational learning to occur it must be done as a series of steps: exposure, acquisition and acceptance. Exposure is defined as the observer witnessing the modeled behavior. The second step, acquisition, occurs when the individual retains the knowledge presented by the model. Acceptance, the final step, only happens if the new knowledge changes the behavior of the observer. Modeling therapy can be successfully used with autistic children. First, the child is shown a social behavior such as two people shaking hands on a video. Next, the therapist shapes the child's hand into a handshake position and shakes the child's hand. Over many trials the child will learn how to imitate directly from the video and begin to model behaviors by themselves.

Operant conditioning therapies

There are several terms that should be defined before explaining the methods of operant conditioning therapy. Operant is behavior that an individual does which changes their surroundings in some measurable way. If what happens is good the behavior is "reinforced" and the individual will probably do that behavior more. If what happens is bad the behavior is "punished" and the individual will probably not do that behavior again. According to their theoretical background counselors approach operant conditioning therapy in a variety of ways. Traditional psychotherapists want the client to understand why they behave as they do. Operant orientated therapists believe that the behavior is the problem and try to help the client learn better ways of responding to stimuli. Behavior therapists only deal with behaviors that are measurable, like drinking too much alcohol. Behavior therapists may decide an individual is doing something too much, behavioral excess or not enough, behavioral deficit.

Positive reinforcement

Operant conditioning therapies often use positive reinforcement to help the client change specific behaviors. A positive reinforcement is a type of reward. In order to have the most effect positive reinforcement must be given immediately after the behavior happens. If the individual can't or won't do the behavior at all a therapist can use "shaping" to produce the behavior. For example if an older child refuses to use the toilet then a shaping system using stickers may be devised. First, the child would receive a sticker for entering the bathroom, after a time the child would have to sit on the toilet to receive a sticker; finally the child would earn a sticker only for using the toilet properly. Eventually, usually within a few weeks the client will begin to perform the desired behavior without reward.

Extinction and punishment

Sometimes operant conditioning therapies are used to make an individual stop doing a bad behavior. In this case either extinction or punishment is used in the therapeutic process. Extinction is used to stop bad behavior when the reinforcer, the thing that encourages the individual to continue the behavior, can be found and stopped. For example, if a child refuses to go to bed when asked to by her parents it might be found that the parents are reinforcing the behavior by giving in to her pleas for "one more story". In order to get the child to bed on time the parents must stop giving in to her requests. Punishment can be used to stop bad behavior by giving a negative response to an individual when they do the bad behavior or by taking away something that the individual likes. An example of negative response punishment is if a parent put the child in a corner after the child uses naughty language. An example of taking something away would be reducing television time if the child is refusing to complete homework.

Pavlovian conditioning

Ivan Pavlov developed Pavlovian conditioning in Russia in the early 1900's. Pavlovian conditioning is also sometimes called "respondent" or "classical" conditioning. This conditioning takes an unconditioned response (UR) which is usually brought about by an unconditioned stimulus (US) and creates a condition where the UR is brought on by a conditioned stimulus (CS) and renamed the conditioned response (CR). In the famous Pavlovian example of dogs salivating when they heard a specific sounds: food was the unconditioned stimulus, salivating was he unconditioned response, the sound was the conditioned stimulus, and salivating then became the conditioned response. Research has shown that Pavlovian conditioning can be used to work with people. Systematic desensitization is one type of therapy which arose from Pavlovian conditioning. Pavlovian conditioning is very similar to reinforcement, except that the stimulus is always given in Pavlovian conditioning regardless of the behavior performed.

Person-centered therapy

Person-centered therapy created by Carl Rogers emphasizes the way a person behaves rather than why a person behaves in a particular way. Rogers believed that individuals place themselves at the center of their own personally defined universe and that the self is constantly making small adjustments based on incoming information. Person-centered therapy declares that the only to treat an individual is to view the world through them. Mental illness is said to be an imbalance in the "self" and the individual's actual experiences. Another important part of Roger's theory is self-actualization and congruence. Self-actualization is defined as becoming "a fully functional individual". The individual who is self-actualized is creative, present minded and makes decisions without fear or regret. Congruence is the process of communicating truthfully and easily with other people.

Carl Rogers developed a seven stage therapy involving his theory of person-centered therapy.
- An individual at stage one avoids personal discussions and intimate relationships.
- Stage two is marked by the individual beginning to open up or admit that they have problems.
- Stage three sees the individual begin to wonder whether their beliefs are rational.
- In stage four the person admits they have feelings and talks about them a little; they also begin to take responsibility for themselves.
- Eagerness to become the real self begins in stage five. Also in stage five people fin that having feelings and talking about them is perfectly natural and normal.
- At stage six the individual opens up to the possibility of being their true self while engaged in an intimate relationship.
- The final stage, stage seven, is marked by complete self-actualization.

Play therapy

Play therapy is of special interest to social workers who typically have children for clients. Usually play therapy is done on a one-to-one basis; however it may be used within the process of family therapy as well. While playing the children learn how to better control their emotions, the difference between right and wrong, and a number of cognitive skills. The child decides what to play with and any rules associated with the play. The social worker watches and listens carefully in order to asses the child's problems and coping mechanisms. Sometimes the counselor may play along with the child helping them to make good decisions. Play therapists may use dolls, puppets, toy vehicles, or any number of "open ended" toys that can be played with in a creative and expression filled manner. Perhaps the most important element of play therapy is the bond of trust created between child and counselor as well as unconditional acceptance on the part of the counselor.

Rational emotive therapy

Albert Ellis developed rational emotive therapy (RET) in 1955. In 1989 Ellis defined six fundamental ideas about RET.
- The tendency to be rational or irrational is present at birth.
- Irrational thinking can be made stronger by contact with family and society.
- An individual must think before he can feel or act.
- RET therapists should be the voice of reason for the client and should not attempt to develop a "warm fuzzy" relationship with the client.
- RET therapists should use many strategies to encourage their clients to change the way they think in order to relieve symptoms.
- The way people view the world and hold unrealistic beliefs is the cause for all emotional problems.

The four steps of RET are as follows:
- the client is taught to recognize thoughts as being rational or irrational
- the client is shown how their emotional problems are merely a symptom of their faulty belief system
- the client is taught how to replace irrational thinking and illogical beliefs with an appropriate way to think

- the client learns how to sue the scientific method and logic to continue to improve their life.

Reality therapy

Reality therapy was developed by William Glasser on the premise that people behave inappropriately because they are not getting one or more of the following needs met: belonging, power, freedom, fun and survival. Reality therapy is quite different than other types of counseling in that:
- it does not believe in "mental illness" or in labeling clients
- it is completely present focused
- it does not feel that transference is part of therapy
- finds the idea of behavior based on the subconscious absurd
- is interested in whether a behavior is right or wrong
- the goal is for people to get their needs met.

Reality therapy is good because it does not take a long time, is easy for a counselor to learn and use, places responsibility on the client and can be used in many different environments.

There are eight stages in reality therapy.
- First, the counselor becomes friends with the client and directly questions the client as to what they want from therapy.
- Next the counselor asks the client to think only about their current behavior.
- Third, the counselor works with the client to look at the behavior realistically.
- Next, they devise a program that will allow the client to get what they need by behaving better.
- The client must then promise to follow the program exactly.
- The counselor will not listen to any reason that the program hasn't been followed.
- However, the client will not be chastised or otherwise punished if the program isn't followed.
- Last, the counselor cannot end therapy until the client is completely better.

The fourth step in which a program is devised is perhaps the most important part of reality therapy. By making the client sign a written contract it puts them, rather than the counselor, in control of their life.

Specific situations

Addiction

There are a number of conduct and deportment characteristics to watch for if a social worker suspects that a client has an alcohol or drug abuse problem. Conduct to be watched for on the job or within the home are as follows:

- the caliber of work changes from one day to the next
- inability to concentrate
- missing work more often
- endangers the safety of self or other
- takes longer lunch breaks and leaves earlier.

Deportment to be watched for on the job or within the home are as follows:

- trouble with money
- stays away from friends and coworkers
- unwilling to accept responsibility
- no longer takes care of how they look
- makes excuses that seem phony.

After abuse has been confirmed a well planned intervention is necessary. The following tips are helpful when planning interventions:

- stay in charge
- stay on topic
- keep written records of proof to use during the intervention
- talk about the conduct and deportment problems not the addiction
- be considerate but firm
- explain were and how they can get help.

Special needs children

Children with special needs, including autism, mental retardation, and developmental delays may be helped with behavioral and educational interventions. Communication and social interactions are often problems for special needs children however there are a number of techniques that can be used to help them improve. In order to use these techniques the child's problem must be clearly defined and easily noticed. The technique chosen must be used consistently by all involved. If the parents are bending the program's rules at home then the child will not get markedly better. Also the child must receive a reward or punishment that has a strong meaning for them. For example taking away television time from the child who would rather be reading anyway would not be a strong enough punishment to change the child's problem behavior.

Sensory integration problems

The sensory integration theory looks at the causes for communication difficulties within the individual's nervous system. The nervous system may malfunction in getting the sensory input from the source (eyes, ears, mouth, etc) to the brain or the malfunction may occur as the brain attempts to process the stimuli into meaningful data. A number of techniques are used with children that often resemble play in order to improve their nervous system function. For example children who have problems with sight may do dot-to-dot games or build houses out of plastic bricks. When working with children who have a particularly over-stimulated sense of touch it is important to remember that it is easier for the child to initiate the touch, that firm pressure is accepted more readily than soft touching and that each child is likely to have one or more things they find particularly difficult to handle.

Aggression

It is commonly believed that aggressiveness is an inherited trait that can be influenced by exposure to aggression at a young age. One process that can be used to reduce aggression is known as "cover assertion". Using covert assertion an individual is taught to control aggression by stopping thoughts of anger and instead think of something calming. This process must be practiced on a regular basis in order to become proficient and to keep a high level of proficiency. The "aggression stimulants structure" asks the client to list the people and situations that make them angry and to think about what would happen if they actually went through with the aggressive behavior. This helps the client to become more aware of their feelings and to take responsibility for their actions. Instructional that emphasizes personal control over anger and stress are particularly helpful in job settings.

Illness, pain and loss

Chronic illness: Individuals who have been diagnosed with a chronic illness they will most likely choose between a problem-focused and an emotion-focused plan in order to deal with the knowledge depending on whether they are used to solving problems in a rational or emotional manner. Individuals who work form a problem-focused mindset seek solutions that will better their long term health, become as knowledgeable about the disease as possible and actively work to reduce tensions surrounding the diagnosis. Individuals who work form an emotion-focused mindset seek to change their internal feelings and learn to accept the diagnosis while focusing on the positive side of life. Some theories argue that all individuals use both problem-focused and emotional-focused strategies to some degree to cope with chronic illness. It is important for the social worker to understand which strategy or combination of the strategies her client is operating under in order to treat them most effectively.

Terminal illness: Individuals who have been diagnosed with a terminal illness face a very large amount of stress as they know that the illness will result in death. Elisabeth Kübler-Ross formulated a five step progression that individuals go through after being diagnosed with a terminal illness in order to arrive at acceptance. The first step is denial. The individual believes that they simply can not be dying. The second step is anger. They may shout at loved ones or caregivers, cry often and or engage in reckless activities. The third step is bargaining. Bargaining sees the individual trying to negotiate with "higher powers". For example the individual may say, "God if you will let me live another year I will devote fifty percent of my waking hours to feeding the poor." Not all individuals experience this step. The fourth step is depression. This step arises when the individual begins to mourn for lost chances. They may feel unhappy that they can no longer perform a specific task. The final step is acceptance. It is with acceptance that the individual understands that death is inevitable and cannot be forestalled.

Pain management: The process of pain management varies greatly depending on the type of pain, cause of pain, the individual experiencing pain and culture. For example, some cultures believe that pain is to be experienced without complaint or interventions; other cultures use "natural" products to reduce pain, while still other rely on drugs. Individuals with mental illness usually have a lower tolerance to pain than healthy individuals. There are many ways that a social worker can help his clients deal with pain. For pain that is chronic biofeedback can be very helpful. Biofeedback teaches the client to recognize their body's responses to pain and how to manage them. Cognitive therapy is another way to place pain control in the hands of the patient. Cognitive therapy teaches the client how to manage pain with relaxation techniques, distraction, and positive imagery. However, operant therapy does not try to manage the pain itself but instead to get the client to perform a full range of behavior despite the pain.

Phases of grief: John Bowlby developed the idea that normal grief occurs over four phases which are not mutually exclusive and do not necessarily occur in order.

- The first phase, numbing, typically lasts from only a few hours to as much as a week. Numbing is characterized by extreme anguish and fury.
- The second phases, yearning and searching, can go on for years. It is in this phases that the individual desperately wishes to be able to regain what they have lost and attempts to find it.
- The third phase is disorganization and despair. Individuals feel that they will never be happy again and can't seem to "get their act together" while in this stage.
- The final stage is reorganization. Reorganization allows a person to continue grieving but the grief no longer overwhelms them or disturbs their life to a detrimental extent.

Decision making

The social worker who understands how individuals make decisions will be better equipped to help his clients work through their problems in a direct rational manner. First, the social worker must understand the concept of heuristics. Heuristics are the factors a person uses to accept or throw out various solutions to problems. The decision theory of decision making takes into account likelihood and utility in order to get the most from the final decision. However, there are many more factors which go into decision making than just likelihood and utility. Most studies in decision making today try to take into account the factors which lead from a set number of alternatives to the actual solution chosen. The factor which leads people to make faulty decisions is estimation. People often rely on estimations even in areas were estimates are not the best way to make decisions.

Decision making in regards to motivation

Oftentimes individuals make decisions based on personal motivation. Motivation is typically driven by what the individual expects to happen as a result of his decision and how the consequences will directly affect them. For example despite the continued threat of HIV infection some people continue to engage in high risk sexual practices. An individual may make the decision to continue their risky behavior despite the warning because they believe that a cure for HIV will be found long before they contract the disease. Another individual may realize the risks involved but believe they would never contract the disease themselves. In the first scenario the individual is basing his decision on the idea that an HIV positive status will not be personally harmful. The second individual is basing her decision on the expectation that she is safe and cannot get the disease.

Interventions with couples and families

Family stages

Child development follows along according to the con-concurrent family stage. The first stage in family life concerning children is the image-making stage. This stage occurs during the woman's pregnancy and concerns the two individuals beginning to see themselves as a family rather than just as a couple.

The second family stage is nurturing and begins with the birth of the child and lasts approximately until the child's second birthday. This stage is focuses on the healthy mental, physical and cognitive growth of the child. Often times the parents may feel their roles of "mother" and "father" supplanting their roles of "wife" and "husband" because of the amount of time that is taken up with nurturing the child.

The third stage of parenthood is the authority stage. This stage happens during the child's pre-school years. It is during this time that parents must allow the child room to grow while placing limits.

The fourth stage that a family undergoes is the interpretive stage which begins when a child enters school and ends in early adolescence. Children in this stage are more influenced by other children even tough parents may try to continue to shelter them. Identity formation marks the child's emphasis during the teen years. Parents must now learn how to act as their child's partner. Typically between the ages of 18 and 25 the child enters the launching stage in which the parental role is seen as easing their children away from the family and into the wider world.

MRI theory of family therapy

The Mental Research Institute (MRI) intractional view is one type of family therapy. This model places emphasis on the way problems are mishandled. It states that small problems are often blown out of proportion in the family setting while large problems are ignored. Therapy within the MRI framework works to find solutions to get rid of stress brought on by mishandling problems. Paradoxical procedures, also known as reverse psychology, are the primary therapy technique used in the MRI model. Rather than give the family new coping strategies they are told to continue their ineffective ones. This leads the family to a heightened awareness of both the triggering problem as well as the symptomatic behavior.

Strategic approach to family therapy

The strategic approach to family therapy is almost the direct opposite of the Mental Research Institute (MRI) interactional model. Rather than hoping to change family behavior through paradoxical procedures, Jay Haley and Cloe Madanes believed in assigning special work to be done outside of the therapy session in the home. They also felt that families continue improper behavior because it serves some purpose for the workings of the family. Key to the strategic approach is a specific therapy must be assigned to each specific problem and that no one is alone at fault for mental illness rather it is a family illness and method of coping. To practice this approach the family should be studied for many months before beginning to make diagnosis and prescribe solutions.

Milan systemic family therapy model

The Milan systemic family therapy model is quite different from other types of family therapies. This therapeutic model was first proposed by Mara Selvini-Palazzoli, Luigi Boscolo, Gianfranco Cecchin and Guiliana Prata in Milan, Italy. This therapy is used successfully to help a number of severe illnesses. The cornerstone of this model is the spacing of therapy sessions one month apart over the course of one year, known as "long brief" therapy. The most unique feature of this model is that while one therapist would lead the family therapy session a number of other therapists would watch the session behind a two-way mirror. Occasionally the observing therapists would stop the session to meet with the leading therapist. During these meetings they would discuss intervention ideas.

Behavioral family therapy

Behavioral family therapy is typically used to treat parent-child strife, but may be used for other family problems as well. This therapy has the following four processes that the social worker leads the family member through:

- defining the problem
- family, or in the case of young children parent, education
- individualized plan of treatment
- end of treatment assessment.

In order to define the problem as specifically as possible the family must talk about the following:

- what triggers the questionable act
- the family's reaction to the questionable act
- how often the questionable behavior happens
- how intense the questionable behavior is.

It is also a good idea for the social worker to watch the family in action to be sure of the nature of the questionable act and the possibility of the family unknowingly reinforcing it.

Problem-solving therapy

A therapy which can be used with families, children, adolescents and all other ages is called "problem solving". Problem solving therapy has both a narrow focus, helping the client to solve the exact problem that brought them to the counselor and a wide focus, teaching the client skills which can be used to solve problems in general. This therapy has a strictly controlled regimen of actions that must be followed through in order. First, the client must admit he has a problem and that it is solvable. Second, the client should determine his long term therapeutic goal. Next, the client writes out all the solutions he can think of. He then considers the good and bad points of each listed solution and ranks them from "most likely to work and easiest to carry out" downward. Next, he tries out his highest ranked solution. Finally, with the counselor's help the client examines the outcome and decides if any part of the exercise should be tried again so that a better solution can be found.

Couples therapy

Due to rising divorce rates and second marriages couples therapy has become a large area of practice for social workers. The most common reasons that couples seek therapy for are the inability to communicate well with one another and as a result have difficulty in resolving conflicts. Typically marriage counseling involves both individuals (conjoint therapy) though it may occasionally proceed with only one person alone (individual therapy) or with each individual seeing the counselor in separate sessions (concurrent therapy).

Philip and Marcy Bornstein put forth a five stage model for marriage counseling. These stages are:
- meeting the clients, assessing the problem and taking a history
- teaching the clients how to work together
- educating the clients in proactive communication techniques
- teaching the couple how to resolve problems with each other
- working to keep the couple moving in a positive direction.

Interventions for groups

Group reward

Robert Slavin came up with two types of cooperative learning which use group reward rather than individual reward. Student teams achievement divisions (STAD) works by basing scores for the group on individual improvement. Teams-games-tournament (TGT) pits groups against one another with the highest grade going t the team member whose team wins the game. Studies have shown that students from different racial backgrounds perform better in one type of classroom than another. African American students perform best in the pure cooperative environment of STAD. American children of European decent perform best in the mixed cooperative-competitive environment of TGT. In classrooms where STAD is utilized students make friends from a more wide variety of others which leads to increased social change and a more positive environment for all students.

Crowd behavior

Crowds are groups of people who do not necessarily have underlying bonds but come together for a brief amount of time. A person who is said to be "caught up" in a crowd may behave very differently than if in a small group or alone. Though often studied according their adverse behavior crowds can also be a force for good. Eugene Tarrow defined two phases of crowd behavior: individual and conforming. Within the individual phase people are focused on their identity separate from the crowd. In the conforming phase people begin to act together or mimic the behavior of the majority. Generally crowds can be seen as being violent, apathetic or pro-social. Research has shown that the more anonymous a person feels the more violent they will act in a crowd. Anonymity may be obtained through darkness, large numbers of people, or uniforms. Apathetic crowds can often be explained by the bystander effect which states that the more people who witness an even the less likely any one individual will respond to the event.

Group decision making

Knowledge of group decision making is especially important for social workers who work in community settings. Ivan Steiner defined three important areas in group decision making. The first area is how well the group breaks a large task into individual jobs in order to make it easier to complete the task. The second area is what the final objective is. The final area of importance is the rules by which the group operates under. Steiner also defined the "choice shift" as the difference between what decision an individual makes and what decision is made by the group. Usually groups make decisions that are more severe than decisions made by a single person. In order for groups to arrive at the best possible solution it is important that group members are not influenced by extraneous information or individual preferences. It is also important for group members to be happy about the final decision and feel that it was truly the best solution for the group.

Group counseling

Group counseling grew out of the need to counsel an overwhelming number of people in the years following World War II. Work with groups can be divided into two different fundamental styles: group counseling and group therapy. Two types of group counseling are preventative and developmental Preventative group counseling helps teach life skills in order to avert serious problems from developing. Counseling a group of newly wedded couples on communication skills would be an example of preventative counseling. Developmental group counseling concerns mentally healthy individuals who are striving for personal growth. Group counseling can be effective even if the individual does not speak but actively listens. One disadvantage is that it can be difficult to speak in front of people that you may not completely trust.

Group therapy

Group therapy is for people who realize that they have a problem and want help to learn a more functional way of life. Groups usually have four to twelve individuals who are suffering from the same or similar problems. Also, there may be one or two therapists involved with the group. There are advantages of group therapy for both the clients and the counselor. Some people get better faster when working in a group setting and because a number of individuals are paying for the counselor's time it is far less expensive than one on one therapy. The counselor's time is well spent as they are able to help greater numbers of people than they could otherwise.

Group session

When speaking about group therapy a session is a predefined number of group meetings. Within a session a group will move through five stages. The first stage is orientation. Members of the group must learn to trust one another before they can move on to deeper levels of the reasons why they came for counseling. The individuals must feel that group therapy is a "safe" place to talk about their problems. Once members being to open up a little the group enters the transitional stage. It is now that the individual must take the difficult step of revealing personal information about themselves. The third stage known as cohesiveness and openness features the group member talking about the full extent of their problems. Stage four is behavior modification. In this stage the members try out various ways to change their actions so that they can overcome their problems. The final stage is completion. This final group meeting allows members to express how the group has helped them and how they will continue to improve after the group has finished its work together.

Formal groups

Groups are defined as a number of people who have something in common and may be formal, a college fraternity for example, or informal, 30 individuals viewing a dolphin performance. According to Bruce Tuckman formal groups follow a set path in their development. First, individuals get to know each other, decide who should be included and who should be excluded from the group, and what the group will do. Another stage in group development is when members fight with one another, become unhappy with the group, or attempt to hold certain coveted positions. This stage of disagreeableness is at odds with a time in which decisions are made, problems resolved and solutions agreed upon. Following this stage is the time that groups begin to work together to complete the specified goals. Finally, sometimes a group is no longer functioning properly or is no longer needed and so the individuals go their separate ways.

Group topography

Group topography is defined by how the group looks physically. The basic features of groups are: size, composition, simplifying complexity, density, cost and benefits. The average group size that people use everyday is between three and seven. However, four size categories for groups are generally recognized as:

- small primary groups (2-20 people)
- small nonprimary groups (3-100 people)
- large groups (1,000-10,000 people)
- largest groups (more than 10,000 people).

Group density

Group density should be considered when a group is deciding on a place to hold regular meetings. Density specially refers to the amount of physical space an individual has to himself. Density can be seen as a function of social dimensions (the number of people in a given space) or physical dimensions (the room size needed for a certain amount of people). When individuals feel they don't have enough space they become unhappy, angry, and stressed.

Group composition

Composition refers to the number of one to one relationships possible in any group. The more people that belong to a group the more one to one relationships are possible. As a group gets bigger it gets harder to know everyone. Generally a large group will unconsciously divide itself into subgroups in an effort to simplify complexity. For example, men may drift to the other men in a mixed group of males and females or people may subgroup themselves by age. This sub-grouping tends to make a minority feel more important and get more attention from the group as a whole. By banding together their unified "voice" is louder in the midst of the crowd.

Costs and benefits of being a group member

Costs of membership in a group does not refer only to annual dues. An individual most give up a piece of himself in order to become a member of a group. Generally the larger the group the less of an individual a person becomes. Working with a group may also cost a person time as a task may take longer for a group to complete than for an individual to finish. In the case of school children working with a group may also bring lower grades. On the other hand there are many benefits for being part of a group. Being a group member gives an individual a social network which can improve a person's health and well being. Some groups are purposefully designed to help members lower stress or overcome obstacles. Membership in a group may also confer status.

Interventions with communities

Strategic negotiation

Strategic negotiation is a means to work out short term individual goals which conflict with long term community goals. Strategic negotiation works on a system of offers and counter offers similar to bargaining. First, all community members should invited to an information hearing were all pertinent information regarding the conflict is given by a social worker or mediator. Afterward individuals are allowed to speak either on their own behalf or on behalf of the group. At a future date negotiations are held either in real time or through letters. Soft negotiators are those who will give up some of their self-interests in the interest of the community. Hard negotiators stand firm and are unwilling to give in even a small amount.

Even for long term community goals it is impossible to say whether hard or soft negotiating is best for achieving the desired outcome.

Effective negotiation

Roger Fisher and William Ury developed a four step model of effective negotiation called "principle negotiation". This type of negotiation should work for the smallest one-on-one disputes up to and including cases where entire countries or world regions are attempting to bargain with one another. This seemingly simple task allows the involved parties to feel that they are working together to defeat a common problem rather than looking out for their own personal interests. Step two involves declaring any latent concerns that should be resolved before taking on the main problem. The third step is the time for all parties to brainstorm possible solutions. In this step they are able to work together to find solutions that would benefit everyone. Step four requires that the chosen solution be considered fair and binding by all parties. Using principled negotiation allows for a win-win situation without any one group conceding to another.

Jigsaw learning

Generally there are two ways for people to work: competitively and cooperatively. Jigsaw learning is a type of cooperative work created by Elliot Aronson and is used to foster a sense of community within the educational environment. While jigsaw learning can be used in schools, universities, businesses and other groups it is perhaps most easily illustrated using a class of middle school students. For example, the teacher announces that the next test topic will be World War II. Then the teacher forms groups of students from a variety of backgrounds to work together. Within each group each individual will take on a different subtopic such as famous battles, daily life in England, Anne Frank, etc. Individuals then meet with those students who share their subtopic before reporting back to their original group. After a specified time period students are tested individually about World War II as a whole. Jigsaw learning does have its problems though as if one individual is unwilling to work hard his laziness will bring down the scores of other group members.

Social support

Sidney Cobb defined social support as, "the receipt of information that one is cared for, is valued and belongs to a mutually supportive social network." Individuals may view social support in one of five ways:

- the feeling that other people regard the individual in a good way
- bonds based on mutual credence or sentiment
- being given physical objects or help that the person needs
- the belief that the individual does not have to face a bad situation without support
- having someone willing to listen in a non-judgmental way to the individual's thoughts and feelings.

Research has shown that social networks are very important to the outcome of a diagnosed illness. Illnesses ranging from cancer to depression have a higher rate of recovery in individuals with the belief that they have support from others. This may be because the social network acts as a cushion between the individual and stress or because people with social networks generally have a high level of optimism.

Communication

Principles

Language

According to the *American Heritage Dictionary* language is defined as the communication of thoughts and feelings through a system of arbitrary signals, such as voice sounds, gestures, or written symbols. Every language must have rules and be methodic in order to function properly. Language may take the form of speech, writing, hand gestures, and body movements. There are four primary factors in language: phonology, semantics, grammar and pragmatics. Phonology is the practice of using phonemes, the smallest units of speech which can change the meaning of a word. For example "queen" has three phonemes "qu", "e", "n". Semantics is broken down further into two subsystems: lexical and grammatical. A word's definition is derived from lexical semantics. Grammatical semantics uses the system of morphemes the smallest units of language which have a meaning all their own. For example "queens" has two morphemes, "queen" which means a female ruler and "s" which means more than one. Morphology and syntax make up the factor of grammar. Morphology are those rules which govern sentence formation. Pragmatics deals with the everyday use of language.

Linguistics

Linguistics is a scientific pursuit to determine how language is arranged. Linguistics studies how well a person understands language, how individuals learn language, and how spoken language is thought of by an individual. Noam Chomsky developed a breakthrough theory in linguistics when he stated that language is genetically coded for within each person. He also stated that there are a number of "linguistic universals" which all languages share. This theory was in direct opposition to that of B. F. Skinner who believed language was learned. Further research into the field of linguistics has in fact bolstered both theories though specifying that some parts of language are inborn while others are learned. It is also been shown that while other animals may have simplistic forms of language or may be taught forms of human language the language of humans is far more complex than that of other animals.

Feedback and evaluation

Two important parts of communication are feedback and evaluation, each of which can be done formally or informally. These types of communication are especially important in teacher-student and supervisor-trainee relationships. Feedback is non-judgmental allowing the individual receiving it to heighten their level of self-awareness. Evaluation is judgmental and follows a list of behaviors that the individual receiving it should be doing to a specific level of competence. Formal feedback is given in writing, notes in the margin of a writing assignment suggesting changes for example. Informal feedback takes the form of spoken observations without letting the individual know if the behavior was good or bad. Formal types of evaluation are test scores and grades. Informal evaluation is spoken praise or disapproval.

Visual communication

Visual communication is a very important part of communicating information. People usually remember up to 10% more when both hearing and seeing information over just hearing it. It is often easier to illustrate complicated information than to try to explain it. Visual communication can be formatted so that speakers of different languages can understand the material easily. Also visual information gathers the audience's attention. Be sure that the visual is professional in appearance and that its tone matches that of the information. For example cartoons would most likely be inappropriate during a grieving workshop. Practice the presentation with the visual aids in the presentation room whenever possible in order to be most comfortable with it and to be sure that all of the necessary equipment functions properly.

Written communication

Writing is perhaps the most difficult form of communication. Writing well takes many hours as the writer must make many drafts in order for the finished product to be polished and professional. It is important not to be "wordy" and to use clear precise language. Written communication is especially appropriate when the communicator and receiver need to have a copy of the information for future reference because the mater is difficult to understand at first approach, the information includes explicit instructions and/or for legal purposes. Written information is cheaply an easily given to many people at one time. The drawbacks of written communication include the time involved in production and the lack of immediate feedback for the writer.

Interpersonal communication

There are four principle truths in interpersonal communication. First, it is impossible to be completely uncommunicative. It is important for social workers to remember that even if an individual refuses to engage in active communication they are communicating something through the refusal. Once communication has been received it can not be rescinded by the communicator. Remember to think before speaking. Also, communicating with other people is highly complex. Because a person can never truly know another person's thoughts all communication is filtered through personal interpretations. This is especially important to remember when working with multicultural clients. Finally there are a number of contexts that guide communication. These contexts include the relationship between the individuals communicating and where the communication is occurring.

Five contextual factors of interpersonal communication

There are five contextual factors which impact interpersonal communication. The first context is psychological. This factor includes the "who" of the individuals involved in a conversation. Whether or not one person has had enough sleep or is depressed or in an optimist are just a few examples that impact the psychological factor. The second context is relational. This factor concerns the attitude of the individuals toward one-another. For example, is one person the student of the other? The third factor involves the psych-social "where" of the conversation and is known as situational. A boss speaking to an employee in the office has a different situational context then the same two people talking at the beach. The fourth factor, environmental, explains the physical "where" of the communication. These contexts include time and temperature. Finally the fifth factor involves cultural contexts which are behaviors learned in society.

Crises communication

Communicating competently during a crisis takes preparation and planning. In social work practice the association should have solid plans in place for various types of mental health crises. A good crises communication plan should involve the entire association including social workers, secretaries and supervisors. The following are essential to good crises communication:

- speak clearly and truthfully
- be empathetic, talk about what can be done to help the problem and what can be done to prevent the problem from re-occurring in the future
- respond to each issue of trouble as soon as it happens
- let other people on the scene know as much as possible
- do not become inpatient as it will worsen the situation for everyone involved.

Interactional view of communication

The interactional view of family communications assumes that change can only occur with help from a social work counselor. This theory has five axioms. The first axiom, "one cannot not communicate," means that even silence sends a message. The second axiom, "human beings communicate both digitally and analogically," means that people use both symbols (analogs) and words (digital) to send information. Axiom three states, "communication = content + relationship". Content is what a person means to say while relationship is how the person says it. The fourth axiom says, "The nature of the relationship depends on how both parties punctuate the communication sequence." This axiom refers to how an individual expresses feelings from one interaction to the next. Finally axiom five states, "All communication is either symmetrical or complementary." Symmetrical communication occurs when both people have equal power. Complementary communication occurs when one person has more power than the other.

Good communication

The following is a list of behaviors which are the trademarks of a social worker with good communication skills:

- polite
- always on time
- speaks personally to the client
- uses everyday language
- listens well
- thinks before speaking
- careful to explain what is occurring and why

- keeps promises
- honest
- patient with clients
- makes no assumptions based on outward appearance alone
- chooses the place of communication carefully
- asks for feedback
- uses closed ended questions when necessary
- uses what works best for the client
- works to build a good counseling relationship
- remembers the client's English abilities.

Excellent communication requires active listening, appropriate choice of time and place, and adequate self-expression. Active listening involves watching for non-verbal communication and observing underlying meaning. Choice of time and place sued to communicate will vary from client to client. Children tend to communicate better during play rather than when being expected to sit still. Adult clients typically demand a high level of privacy and calm surroundings in order to be open to communication. It is the job of the social worker to assess each client as to the good timing of communication. Adequate self-expression is about more than just word choice. The social worker should be careful with their tone of voice, facial expressions and body language.

Effective communication

As with successful listening, effective communicating must be learned and practiced in order for an individual to become competent in it. In order to communicate well the individual must first be honest with themselves and then tell only the truth to the listener. The speaker should practice what he wants to say ahead of time. One should not give up if the liner doesn't understand right away. Instead he should reword the issue. It is important to speak when calm as effective communication is disrupted by anger. One must keep on task and don't sidetrack as this will confuse the listener. Beginning a sentence wit the word "you" may put the listener on the defensive so it should be avoided whenever possible. In order to keep the conversation about the speaker's issues he should start sentences with "I".

Successful listening

Being a successful listener does not come naturally but must be cultivated and practiced. Good listeners care about the speaker's well being and want to help them. Also, good listeners should never judge the speaker or give advice. Being judgmental shuts the speaker out and giving advice doesn't work because it makes the person feel inferior and allows them to blame someone else for their behavior. Sometimes a good listener should ask questions in order to facilitate the conversation. Never try to tell the speaker that "it doesn't matter". It does matter or the speaker would not be taking the time to tell you about it. Also do not try to explain the problem to the speaker. Only the speaker knows and completely understands the problem.

There are a number of things a social worker can do to improve listening skills. Perhaps the most important thing to remember is that a person can't listen while they are talking. Always wait for the client to speak first. Give the client plenty of time to process what you say excursing patience. Do not try to guess what the client is trying to say or interrupt while they are speaking. Sit close to the client and keep your eyes on them. They will know if you are watching the clock. Be calm and gentle if the client becomes upset or angry. Never punish the client for foul language or loud speech. Finally make sure that the client understands by asking follow up questions and/or observing their behavior.

Conflict resolution

There are six steps which can lead to successful conflict resolution.
- Never try to resolve a problem when angry. Count to 100 or make an appointment to get back the issue.
- Be sure that tall parties involved understand exactly what the conflict is about.
- Decide what is really important to you that you won't compromise on and things that you are willing to give on.
- Bring several options into the conversation. There is almost never one right way to solve a problem so be inventive.
- When you have tried the previous four steps and are still unable to resolve a conflict ask for a mediator to help bring the parties together.

If everything has been tried and does not work ask a disinterested individual to create a binding solution.

Component model of communication

The component model is used to explain communication competence and is defined by three factors. Factor one is knowledge which is the ability to determine which types of communication are appropriate in a given situation. This factor is learned from cultural and societal experience. Factor two is skill. Skills are learned aptitudes. For example all people can speak but taking a class on elocution will dramatically improve a person's ability to speak in public. The last factor is motivation. A person must want to communicate clearly and well in order to do so. Good communication isn't automatic. However, some forms of communication will work for some relationships and not for others which does not imply dysfunction on either group.

Constructivist theory of communication

The constructivist theory of communication developed by Jesse Delia alleges that individuals who think better communicate and understand better. Social workers who ascribe to this theory of communication use the role category questionnaire to try and see how the internal process of communication working for each individual. Individuals may use one of three types of communication according to their abilities. The simplest form of interpersonal communication according to the constructivist theory is expressive design logic and includes little to no thought on the part of the speaker. The conventional design logic includes some forethought by the speaker but the information is presented only from the speaker's point of view. The most complex form of interpersonal communication is rhetorical design logic. This type of communication requires considered forethought by the speaker and works to express both the speaker's and the listener's point of view.

FIRO

The fundamental interpersonal relationship orientation (FIRO) theory was devised by W. C. Shcutz as an explanation for why people enter into relationships. The foundation of FIRO is that all people have three basic interpersonal needs: inclusion, control and affection. The need for inclusion relates to a person's desire to fit in or be a part of the "in" crowd. Inclusion may also be expressed as a wish for other people to be included and not feel lonely. The need for control relates to a person's desire to be the boss or leader of a relationship. On the other side of control are people who try to place others in a possession of power over themselves. Finally is the need for affection which relates to a person's desire to feel love or to give love to other people. The amount and direction of each person's need in regard to the three factors of FIRO stems from childhood experience and is set for life.

Relational dialectics

An interpersonal communication model that looks at how close the relationship becomes is the relational dialectics theory. This theory specifically states that closer relationships are harder to maintain than casual relationships. Couples face stress within the relationship and from outside forces as well. The first stress felt by all couples in "integration versus separation." This stress refers to the amount of time the individual want to spend as a couple (integration) and alone (separation). The second form of stress is "stability versus change". To look for new things (change) is a part of human nature but the couple must also have a strong sense of their relationship (stability) in order to survive. "Expression versus nonexpression" is the final stress factor in relational dialectics. The amount an individual shares (expression) their emotion, thoughts and activities will change depending on the situation. Some people are simply more introverted (nonexpression) than others. It is important that for each stress factor the two opposites balance each other and that the individuals are in close agreement with one another in their preferences.

Mary Ann Fitzpatrick's theory of marital communication

Mary Ann Fitzpatrick based her theory of marital communication on three different types of couple relationships. Couples who are "traditionalists" have probably the strongest relationships as they rely on one another for friendship, advice and stability but are also self assured as individuals. Marriages that are defined as "independent" often revolve around the need for power. Independent couples typically go outside of the marriage for friends, are argumentative and may even have separate bedrooms. Finally couples who live together as "separates" have many short-lasting arguments, go outside of the marriage for advice and find it difficult to express feelings with one another. A couple may move back and forth through the stages depending on the stability of their relationship and the underlying personality of each individual.

Mark Knapp's model of relationship development

Mark Knapp proposed the relationship development model to try and explain how relationships evolve over time. There are two processes and a number of stages within this model. The first process "coming together" outlines the stages involved with relationship formation. These stages are as follows:

- initiating, first contact
- experimenting, getting to know one another
- intensifying, taking the relationship beyond simple friendship
- integrating, having mutual feelings
- bonding, becoming as one.

The second process "coming apart" outlines the stages involved with the dissolution of the relationship. These stages are as follows:

- differentiating, beginning to notice individual differences
- circumscribing, talking around the real issue
- stagnating, lack of communication
- avoiding, trying not to be around one another
- terminating, end of the relationship.

Techniques

Report writing

There are a number of things to keep in mind when writing a report that will allow the social worker to communicate well. First plan the report. Decide why the report is being written, what tone and level of professional language will be used based on who will be reading it, and what response is wanted. Next consider the way in which the paper will be put together. If it is a short report then a title page and list of references is all that is required. Longer reports should also have a table of contents, abstract and final summary. Be sure that the paper is well presented on the page by using double spaces between lines of text, including simple graphs or charts, using bulleted lists and bold headings at the start of each new section. Resist the use of clichés and idioms as they are difficult to translate.

Counseling sessions

It is important to choose the time and place for communication carefully and to match them with the client's needs. There are several things the social worker can do to improve their skill of choosing appropriate communication areas. First, meet the client in a well lit area so that you can be sure that the client can see you. Try not to choose areas which are full of distractions such as a room filled with windows overlooking a busy sidewalk. Choose a location that will be quiet and use soft gentle music (if any) in the background. Make allowances for when the client is most awake and best able to communicate such as early morning for adults or afternoon for adolescents.

Self-expression

Self-expression is not only the words a social worker uses but also how they hold their body, contort the face, and tone of voice. First, plan out what you need to say to the client and the most efficient method for communicating the information. Use short sentence free from professional jargon. Ask only one question at a time. Think about problems that may occur and how you will handle them. Sit on the same level of as the client in a position that will make them feel most comfortable. Never sit behind a desk as this can bring about hostility in the client. Make direct eye contact and be sure that the client is focused directly on you. Use an agreeable calm tone of voice that invites the client to participate in the conversation. Be aware of how you are holding your body and face. Try to retain a relaxed posture and reassuring face.

Playful communication

There are times when a less that serious method of communication is appropriate. Playful communication uses banter to make an individual feel at ease during a conversation. Playful communication can be used between the social work supervisor and the trainee to help ease the trainee's transition into the group and make them feel connected. If used appropriately this style of communication can strengthen the relationship between supervisor and trainee. Certainly the supervisor would not use playful banter during formal evaluation but during informal feedback away from the client or during breaks the use of jokes or funny stories can be appropriate and give the trainee a sense of confidence.

Family communication

Family communication may be difficult to understand by an outsider as it is based on a design created by the family to help them interact with one another and understand the world outside the family structure. Individual mental health depends upon the family working and living well together which in turn depends upon honest communication. The more willing family members are to engage in communication the stronger the family unit becomes. The Family Communication Environment Instrument describes three factors that are a part of family communication. Expressiveness is the first factor and is defined as a willingness to hear the views and emotions of all family members. The second factor which is defined by a husband and wife filling traditional roles while children are expected to comply with family strictures is known as structural traditionalism. The third factor, avoidance, is used by families to stay away from distasteful subjects and maintain assimilation.

Communicate information

There are various ways that a social worker can communicate information. Orally in person or by telephone or written in the form of a letter, report or email are several ways. To decide which method to choose it is important to be aware of a number of things regarding the information. The first thing to decide is the purpose of the information you are giving. Next, decide whether or not the listener should perform something after listening. Then decide if it is necessary to emphasis some parts of the information more than others. Fourth, determine your level of knowledge regarding the information. The next step is to establish whether the information is of a time sensitive nature. Finally consider the client and the way in which they receive and understand best. For example it would be best not to mail an appointment remainder less than one week from the appointment but to telephone instead.

Oral reports

Oral communication is best used when the individual wishes to receive immediate feedback, hold a question-and-answer session, persuade the listener or when the situation is tense. The following, in no particular order, are six areas which should be clearly thought out in order for oral communication to be compelling.
- State an introduction which will grab the audience's attention. Announce the principles, define the problem, mention the objectives and give a brief outline.

- Organize the information in a clear and sensible manner. Also, be sure that the content is sufficient without being overly verbose.
- Use visual aids to help explain particularly crucial or complicated material.
- State a conclusion which adequately summarizes the information. Don't forget to hold a question and answer session.

Be sure that your style of delivery matches the message.

Relationship Issues

Affiliation and friendship

Affiliation is the desire to be around other people. Individuals have different reasons for desiring affiliation which fulfills other needs as well. Fear and the desire to find out if their beliefs are right are two reasons for affiliation. Another type of affiliation is friendship. Generally people become friends because they live close to one another or see each other a lot. This is known as propinquity. Maintaining friendships however is more dependent on how alike two people are and whether or not they find the other person physically appealing. Friendships typically begin as the exchange of one favor for another. Close friendships evolve into partnerships were the giving of favors is seen to benefit the giver as well as the receiver. Other things important to long term friendships are communication and trust.

Motives for affiliation

Individuals tend to form groups in order to stay safe and gain resources. There are many reasons that an individual chooses one group to be a member of over another. Primarily people join a specific group in order not to be seen as an out-cast or social rebel. Another reason to join a group is that the member enjoys doing the same things bowling or quilting for example. A third reason for group affiliation might be for professional gains. Affiliation can be good for society because it can bring people together to form strong alliances but it can be bad for society as well because the purpose of many groups is simply to keep certain people out. Hierarchical divisions within groups can also be positive, for example when older members work to teach the younger members, or harmful, for example when senior fraternity member punish freshmen pledges.

Altruism and non-altruistic motivation

Altruism is defined by the *American Heritage Dictionary* as the "unselfish concern for the welfare of others". Two schools of thought exist as to why people help one another. Some social scientists believe that no act is 100% altruistic and that the individual acts only because of some benefit to herself. This is known as egoistic motivation. Other social scientists feel that individuals act altruistically for a variety of reasons. Cooperation is a good example of behavior that helps both people involved.

The negative state relief theory of helping was developed by Robert Caldini. This type of motivation occurs when an individual feels sad when they see a homeless man. In order to get rid of the sad feelings the individual gives money or food to the homeless man. Another theory of egoistic motivation was developed by Jane Bilavin and is known as arousal-reduction. For example getting a stomach ache when seeing war orphans on TV but when the individual sends money to the orphans the stomach ache goes away. A third type of non-altruistic helping is when the individual behaves in such a way as to gain popularity.

Empathy and altruism

One point of view of altruistic behavior is that it is done on the basis of empathy. If an individual acts on another person's behalf simply for unselfish reasons then this behavior is known as empathy-altruism. Another point of view of altruistic behavior is known as prosocial motivations. According to this theory good behavior towards other people can be increased by giving rewards or by tying the people together with common goals. Another type of prosocial behavior, known as the bystander effect, happens more often if fewer people are present. This may be because the pressure felt by each individual is higher the fewer people are around. This motivation to help people in an emergency appears to be inborn as opposed to helping out a stranger in a non-emergency which is socialized behavior.

Theories of attraction

People often wonder why they are attracted to certain types of individuals. Most theories that deal with attraction emphasize reinforcement as the most important reason people form relationships. Donn Byrne and Gerald Clove developed the reinforcement-affect model of attraction. This theory states that people are attracted to others because the other people reward them in some way or are affiliated with rewards in the individual's mind. For example a child may like the dentist because her mother buys her a movie after each visit to the dentist not because the dentist is nice. The social exchange theory is another model of attraction. This model has the individual weighing the benefits of joining a group versus the negative views of society to that group. Following on social exchange theory is equity theory. The equity theory looks at how both people in a relationship weigh the positives and negatives of being in that relationship.

Mother-child bond

The ethological theory of mother-child attachment was developed by John Bowlby. This theory states that babies are born with the ability to form attachments by exhibiting certain behaviors. There are two basic types of mother-child attachment. Secure attachments are formed by a gentle mother who disciplines with kindness and responds to a child's tears quickly. Babies with secure attachments are not overly fretful when left with a stranger and are happy to see their mother when she returns. Children with secure attachments are happier, have a high level of self confidence and perform better at school than children with insecure attachments. Insecure attachment can be broken into two categories. In avoidant attachment a baby does not respond when mother returns after an absence. In resistant attachment babies are very upset to be left by mother but show no excitement at her return.

Self

There are several theories that try to define the concept of self. Sigmund Freud did not believe in a singular "self" but instead focused on a three part definition known as the "ego, id and superego". Carl Jung defined "self" as a kind of archetype which is inborn with specific potential that is molded by experience. Karen Horney also stated that "self" was inborn but went on to say that everyone is born with a mentally healthy "self" but through anxious experience some people try to become a different "self". Margaret Mahler believed that the "self" does not arise until a child is approximately three years old and has learned to distinguish herself from other people. However, Harry Stack Sullivan believed that the "self" can never be viewed out of context from outside relationships. Finally Heinz Kohut defined the healthy "self" as resulting from positive childhood relationships.

"Self" according to the developmental theories

Developmental theorists focus on the cognitive development of the self. Erik Erikson explained that the ego must go through a number of crises in order to be completely formed. He listed a number of ego developmental stages starting in childhood, autonomy versus shame and doubt for example and continuing until made solid in adulthood. His theory of adolescent identity crises has led to much information about self-esteem. Building on Erikson's work, James Marcia felt that only those adolescents that worked through a period of identity crises would become healthy well rounded adults. If they do not have this chance to learn who they are they will become confused and will not have a good sense of "self".

"Self" as defined by the humanistic and existential theories

The "self" is not as important to humanistic and existential theories as it is in other theories. "Proprium" was used to define the idea of "self" by Gordon Allport. He believed that as a person ages they form a structure of personality. Carl Rogers shunned the notion of "self" as being too simplistic to explain what a human being is. Instead he used the idea of a self-image to represent the entire person's beliefs about themselves. Abraham Maslow defined the idea of the "self" to be apart of an individual's desire for "self-actualization." The concept of being related to the environment that surrounds us as "self" was developed by Rollo May.

"Self" according to Albert Bandura

Albert Bandura felt that the "self" was part of a three part model made up of individual (self), behavior, and environment. The individual takes some control over the behavior which is heavily influenced by the environment. The individual is able to exert this control using self-observation, judgmental processes and self-reaction. Self-observation occurs when the "self" actively looks at what the individual is doing. The next step, judgmental process, decides if the behavior occurring is good, bad or neutral. Finally the self-reaction step is made up of individual rewards or punishments for behavior. Some theorists have divided self-observation from self-conciseness by defining self-observation as looking at one's own thoughts and behaviors and defining self-consciousness as the mount of time a person engages in self-observation.

Self-disclosure

Self-disclosure occurs when an individual relates information of a personal nature to another individual. The closer two people are to one another the more likely they will engage in self-disclosure. Clients in the social work practice should be encouraged to self-disclose and be made to feel comfortable and safe when doing so. One of the social worker's main tasks is to get the client to "open up" and talk about deeper problems and issues. On the other hand self-disclosure on the part of the social worker must be used with great discretion. Before telling a client information of a personal nature the social worker must be sure he has the client's best interest in mind and that the revelations of such information will not harm the client in any way.

Transference and counter-transference

In social work counseling transference can be positive for the client. Transference occurs when the client attributes negative behaviors to the social worker and reacts to the social worker as if she were the person who inflected the pain upon them. As the counseling relationship continues the client should work through these feelings towards the social worker in order to manage the feelings to the true object of the emotions. Counter-transference is the negative feeling a social worker may feel when confronted with the client's transference. The social worker should recognize these feelings and deal with them in an appropriate manner, never allowing the client to see the negative feelings.

Emotions

Emotions can be defined by the following five factors:
- they are encounters not something that is done or thought
- they have "valence", they are not neutral but always positive or negative
- a person must think about their current situation in order to feel emotion
- they involve bodily responses such as frowning or breathing heavily
- they can become stronger or weaker.

Robert Plutchik lists the following eight inborn basic emotions: "joy, anticipation, anger, disgust, sadness, surprise, fear and acceptance". These basic emotions may combine to form more complex emotions. However, most research into emotion focuses only on the basic eight because each person can combine them into a vast variety of complex emotions. For research purposes emotions are divided into "state", what is currently occurring and "trait", the frequency of a particular emotion.

Facial feedback

Several theories exist about the role of facial features in society. Charles Darwin first hypothesized about the universality of facial features in the 1870's which was accredited by research 100 years later. All theories on facial feedback agree to the following three things:
- if a person feels one way but expresses the opposite feeling then the first feeling will decrease
- if a person expresses a facial feature they will begin to feel like that emotion

- the muscles used to form a particular emotion signal the brain about how it should feel.

These ideas have been back up in numerous research studies even though they don't seem to make sense from an intuitive point of view. This research has led to the development of biofeedback mechanisms which can be used in counseling to help a client cope better.

Intimacy

Intimacy is usually defined as a special relationship between two people. In order to experience intimacy a person must reveal important information about themselves and be understanding when listening to important information the other person in the relationship. Nonverbal communication such as kissing or crying with one another often makes a couple more intimate. In order for intimacy to be healthy a person must first have a strong sense of self. This is necessary as in order to gain intimacy a person must give their deepest secrets to another with all its inherent risks. The two main barriers to achieving intimacy are being afraid of self-disclosure and being unwilling to give the time necessary for forming strong intimate bonds.

Professional Values and Ethics

Limits of ethical codes

Ethical codes exist to protect both counselor and client. They are broadly written so that they can remain flexible but because that also makes them open to interpretation problems can occur. Unfortunately not every problem faced in the counseling profession can be solved by using an ethical code; the code can simply never cover every situation.

Making sure that standards are upheld can be problematic since counseling generally takes place in private. Often the client may not be completely informed or understand what is right and wrong in therapy and so may be taken advantage of. If the client does know that something wrong is occurring they may not wish to tell anyone for fear of their problems becoming more widely known.

Ethical codes are written according to the best practice guidelines known at one particular time and therefore must be updated regularly in order to remain pertinent to current practice. Also ethical codes are difficult to use cross-culturally as each culture may vary on ethical beliefs.

Problems that occur within and between codes of ethics

There are two main problems within any particular ethical code and one major problem between two different ethical codes. First, an individual may use a code of ethics as an excuse to maintain bias or discrimination. For example, an individual believes people who speak English as a second language (ESL) are inferior and therefore uses the code of ethics which states that clients should referred if the counselor can not give them adequate language facilitation to keep from seeing ESL clients. Second, there are times when one section of ethical code comes into direct conflict with another section within the same code. For example, most ethical codes state the importance of confidentiality but in another area state that if a patient makes specific threats against a person then the counselor must inform the authorities. In this case the counselor may be confused as to which ethical statement is the most important. Last, is the fact that codes of ethics differ from one professional organization to another. This becomes a problem only if the counselor belongs to more than one such organization.

Decision guidelines for making ethical choices

There are number of important guidelines counselors should follow when making ethical decisions. First, a counselor should be honest with himself as well as with other people. Sometimes it may be necessary for the counselor to undergo therapy himself or ask a colleague to supervise during situations he feels uncomfortable with. Second, is the standard of always trying to do what is best for the client. The counselor should not force his own goals on the client. Third, the professional must always approach the counseling relationship with openness and understanding. Not all clients are easy to work with but a good counselor treats the "ideal client" the same as the "worst client". Finally, the counselor should keep up with the latest edition of ethical codes by making use of continuing education, professional journals and peers.

Van Hoose Paradise model for ethical education

Many educational programs on ethics use the Van Hoose Paradise model for learning ethical behavior. This model is made up of five developmental stages. In the first stage, punishment orientation, a counselor bases their ideas of right and wrong on the accepted practices set by the community. Institutional orientation, the second stage, has the counselor focusing on the guidelines set out by their place of work. The greater good is placed before the individual good in the societal orientation of stage three. IN opposition to the societal stage is stage four, individual orientation, were the needs of the client come before society's. In the final stage, principle, of the Van Hoose Paradise model the counselor no longer needs the input from outside sources of ethics but instead reaches within herself to know what is right.

Situational ethics

In school counseling and ethics

Counselors who work in or for schools have a particularly difficult situation when it comes to behaving ethically. School counselors must balance the needs, ethics and desires of the client (child), employee (school) and guardian (parent). It is very important that counselors who wish to work in school have training in both the specialized ethics of working with children and also training in how to balance the rights of the three parties involved. Universities which offer programs in school counseling should offer classes in ethics directly geared to the particular problems involved. Individuals who are already certified social workers and wish to work in a school environment should refer to their professional organization's code of ethics and take continuing education classes on the problems of school counseling ethical decision making.

In using assessment tools

A counselor should abide by a particular code of ethics when using assessment techniques with their clients. First, the counselor must know how to choose the assessment that will best meet the needs of the client without causing them unnecessary stress or harm. Second, the counselor should understand how to properly use the chosen assessment and be aware of the issues surrounding the interpretation of the test. Third, the counselor must know the background of the test thoroughly in order to make appropriate decisions based on its outcome. It is also very important that the client understands why the assessment was chosen, the rules involved with completing the assessment, how the counselor intends to use the results and what those results mean for them. The misunderstanding of results can cause harm to the client. As with other matters in counseling the client must give their proper consent before the counselor can share the information learned through the assessment.

In the norms and standardization of assessments

When the counselor uses assessments as a means to diagnose psychological problems they must make particular care that the assessment is targeted to their client. Counselor must know the makeup of the sample population for which the assessment bases its norms. If the counselor is working with African American adolescents then they shouldn't use a test which was normed using a majority of Asian Americans aged 30-45. Knowledge of standardization is important for setting the conditions for the assessment to be completed in. Any variation in setting from the standard can result in the results being invalidated. Some clinical assessments require that the client have stayed awake for a long period of time. If the client did not follow these instructions than the outcome of the test will be worthless.

In the administration of assessments

If a computer is used to administer or score a test the counselor must be sure that it is functioning properly and that the test taker is familiar and comfortable with it. A test should not be completed in private by the client unless the instructions specifically require it. The test taker should know that the ideal test environment is and the counselor should note any deviation from it. Finally it is important that counselors use the most to date form of an assessment procedure. When a counselor is given the right to use an assessment they must not violate the terms under which they are held be the test publisher. These include keeping the assessment secure, giving it only to specific clients and not making unauthorized copies.

In client welfare

There are five things that a social worker should do to promote and maintain client welfare. The first goal known as primary responsibility refers to the fact that social workers must respect their clients worth as an individual and aid their well being. Second a social worker must help their clients to become mentally healthy in ways that are positive and that will allow the client to move on without the counselor once therapy is completed. Working together to create a therapy action plan is the third goal towards fostering client growth. When the social worker and client work together to make therapy decisions the client becomes more self-assured. Fourth, social workers must not view the client only as an individual but as a part of a larger family group. Positive support by family can greatly help the client and should be sought out by the social worker. Last, in regards to career counseling the social worker should never encourage a client to take a job outside their comfort zone or above their ability level.

Fees

Dealing with payment can be a difficult ethical problem between counselor and client. It is very important that before treatment begins the prospective client understands how much he can expect to pay and when as well as what will happen if he does not pay. A social worker's fee should depend on their location and client base. If an individual is in need of help and cannot pay it is up to the social worker to help him find an alternative practice. Also social workers should spend some of their time working pro bono. If at all possible goods should not be traded for therapy. If however it is common practice for other professionals in the area to barter and the client asks to do so then arrangements may be made through a detailed written contract.

Termination

Only under certain circumstances can the therapeutic relationship between counselor and client be terminated without initiation by the client. The counselor must never end therapy without warning. For example if a social worker has plans to go on holiday she must make arrangements for her clients to be seen by other professionals or request the client's permission to miss a session. If there comes a time in the counseling relationship that the counselor feels she is no longer an effective advocate for the client she should recommend the client see another social worker. Also it may be necessary to terminate because the client is no longer getting enough from the counseling or is refusing to complete the work necessary for effective counseling.

If the client's therapy is only scheduled for a set number of sessions then the client must be made to understand when termination will occur. If a client stops paying the bills for therapy then termination is necessary.

In record keeping
Client records may be in the form of written notes, voice or video recordings, or electronic media. Keeping records of therapy is required by state law as well as being a matter of ethics. Social workers should check the requirements in their practice area to ensure they are keeping proper records. Records are kept for the client as well as the counselor. Clients have a right to review or have copies of their records. For this reason it is important to make sure that everything contained inside is accurate and will not damage the patient. It is the sole responsibility of the social worker to keep client records secure regardless of how the client information is stored. If therapy is going to be voice or video recorded it is important to receive the client's permission to record before each visit. Any request for the records to be sent or viewed by someone other than the client must be in writing.

Research and consultation
A very important part of social work is research. If a social worker publishes research or case studies on his clients he must be sure that the clients' identities are completely hidden. This may be accomplished in case studies by changing specific identifying factors such as name, age and vocation. In the case of research a number may be assigned to each individual and used in the place of other identifying information. The client's identity may be used if the client reads the information and gives her permission. Sometimes it is necessary to consult with other professionals or agencies regarding the welfare of a client. When this happens it is important to remember that confidential information can only be given to people when absolutely necessary and then only that information that is essential to the consultation. For example the client's name may be clacked out on all shared documents. Also before handing over any client information to another agency it is important to learn the agency's policy towards

confidential information.

Counseling specialties

The first ethical responsibility of all counselors is to read, understand and be familiar with the code of ethics that is used by their professional society, place of business, and state. A counselor must never overstep the limit for which they have been educated. For example, a child welfare counselor should never attempt to counsel geriatric patients. Instead, ethically, the counselor should refer the patient to either a general counselor or a counselor who specializes in geriatric psychology.

From time to time new areas of counseling are formed. A social worker who wishes to practice in a new area must first receive education in the field through classes, seminars or workshops. The recent trend in on-line counseling would be one area that a social worker would need to seek additional information before beginning to practice it.

Qualifications

Qualifications are another important part of professional ethics in social work. Begin qualified for a counseling job is not just about having a diploma. A social worker should be sure that they are trained and experienced enough to take on the job. The amount of training and experience necessary will of course vary from one job position to another so it is up to the social worker to review their qualifications in this area. Becoming a member of a national or international organization for social work is also a step in becoming qualified. Being an association member implies a certain level of ethical and professional standards. When a social worker must hire someone for a job position it is important that the individual meet their own level of qualification for the position.

Advertising practices

While there is not a rule forbidding social workers from advertising there are standards that must be met in order for the advertisement to be considered ethical. First, the advertisement must meet all local, state and national laws regarding deceptive or false advertising. Second, the social worker cannot make use of a degree outside of the counseling filed or obtained from a non-accredited university. For example, Jane Smith as a master's in social work from Florida State University and a PhD in archeology from the University of Florida. When advertising her social work practice she may not use the title Dr. Jane Smith or Jane Smith, PhD. A social worker must never ask a client to speak on her behalf or appear in an ad, because the client might do so only because of the counselor-client position. If someone does speak up for a social worker she must try to be sure that they are telling the truth.

If a social worker maintains a private practice apart from another general position (whether paid or volunteer) the social worker is not allowed to use the general position in any way to lure patients to his private practice. For example, if a social worker volunteers with a teen suicide hotline he cannot tell a caller about his private practice.

When a social worker writes a book or hosts a seminar he is responsible for the accurateness of any advertising for that book or seminar. This rule applies to anything a social worker might create or do outside of his practice that is associated with counseling. Promoting these creations to clients is strictly forbidden as it may make the client feel unreasonable pressure.

Rules on advertising and product promotion extend past the individual social worker and into the field as a whole. A social worker should be sure that false or misleading advertisements about the profession do not occur and should report it if it does. As always it is up to the individual social worker to stay abreast of the latest rules and norms of advertising.

Social work credentials

Credentials are any diplomas, certificates or memberships in professional organizations relating to the field of social work. A social worker must never say he has credentials when he does not and should correct any mistakes made by others in this regard. Often times the agency which gave the credentials will have rules revolving around the misuse of those credentials so the social worker should make himself aware of those rules and abide by them. Likewise a social worker who has particular credentials should never lead people to believe that he is a better counselor than those social workers who do not hold the same or similar credentials. Only titles or qualifications that have a direct influence on counseling may be used in association with the social worker's practice.

Public responsibility

There are several areas of public responsibility in which the social worker must make careful use of ethical guidelines. First, a social worker must not behave or speak in a discriminatory manner towards individuals that they deal with in their role as a professional counselor. Some discriminatory actions include racism, ageism, and sexism. The second area of public responsibility in social work is the proper reporting to third parties. Counselors should always strive to make their reports as accurate and unbiased as possible. A counselor must never lie to a court of law or insurance company in order to help or harm a client. The third public responsibility is in the area of public speaking. Occasionally a social worker may be asked to speak in public on the subject of counseling. When this occurs the social worker must be certain that the information given is up to date, correct and favorable towards the profession.

Responsibility to other professionals

Social workers have a standard of ethical behavior they must follow regarding other professionals. There is more than one accepted theory of mental illness and many models of therapy. A social worker should know and understand the theories and models used by their co-workers. They must also accept the fact that their methods are equally valid and one is not overall better than another. If in the course of counseling a social worker learns that her client is being seen by someone else as well she should ask the client for permission to view the other records. Once permission has been granted the social worker should contact the other professional and work to form a cooperative relationship in order to further the welfare of the mutual client. When a social worker is making statements in public that come from personal opinion they must declare it as such and enforce the idea that the statement is not backed by any professional organization.

Employer- employee relationships

Whether the social worker is the employee or the employer of someone they should be sure that the relationship is well defined and understood by all parties involved. The individuals should also make verbal or written agreements on how the sharing of information will occur as well as who is responsible for the various tasks of running an office. These agreements should be as specific as possible in order to avoid conflict. Social workers should use and undergo regular evaluations based on set standards known to both parties. Any individuals employed by the social worker should be told of any circumstances that could be detrimental to them. The employer is also responsible for the continuing education of employees.

Consultation

Consultation is an ethically difficult procedure to manage as there are many factors involved in it. First, the social worker must decide if consultation is in the best interest of the client. Next, the social worker must choose a professional individual who is competent and also has the best interests of the client in mind. The social worker should never ask someone who may have conflicting interests to consult. If after bringing a consultant in the social worker realizes that the individual is not professionally competent then he should ask other professionals for help. Social workers and social work agencies should maintain a high level of professional competence so that when called upon to consult they will be able to do so without problems occurring. Within the consultation relationship the social worker should be sure that he understand the client and the problem sufficiently and works strictly for the betterment of the client.

Counseling ethics

Counselor educators

Social workers who wish to teach or develop educational materials about the counseling profession should be qualified teachers and counselors. They should be sure to emphasis the ethical and legal areas of social work and present multicultural materials. Within the teacher-student relationship the teacher is in a dominate position of power. Because students may be unaware of this positional power teachers must set clear guidelines regarding the relationship. Ethical guidelines should enforce the professional aspects of the teacher-student relationship. Some other rules of ethical behavior are listed below.

- Students must be given acknowledgment of their help in research.
- Social workers in the role of teacher should not accept family members or close friends as students.
- Teachers must not have sex or other intimate relations with students.

Counselor supervisors

If a social worker wishes to assume the role of supervisor she must follow a set of ethical guidelines. She should have had instruction in the processes of supervision. She should also know her place within the therapeutic framework. Student supervisors should be supervised by a professional at all times. It is the supervisor's role to make sure that the client's welfare is being looked after and that they are receiving a high standard of care. Supervisors who feel their students are not ready to become certified social workers should help them to gain the necessary skills. Only once a supervisor believes a student is fully qualified can the supervisor recommend the student for certification.

Counselor education

Social workers who plant to teach a course on counseling should be sure that students understand what the course will cover before they enroll.

- The students should be aware of the kind and degree of difficulty of the information they will need to learn in order to pass the class.
- Students should know exactly what areas of counseling will be included in the course.
- Students should understand how they will be graded.
- The students should realize that counseling education fosters self reliance.
- The ways in which they will be supervised and the type of places that they will be allowed to participate in practical learning will be fully disclosed to the students.
- Knowledge of how they will evaluate their teacher and supervisors.
- The students should be aware of the rules which lead to being thrown out of the class.

Students should be told how the class will help them to find a job in the field of social work.

Teachers

When teaching courses in social work there are a number of ethical responsibilities for the instructor to uphold.

- All social work programs should include scholastic studies and field practice.
- Evaluation should be informative, supportive and regularly scheduled.
- The instructor must be sure that students know and understand the ethics involved with social work.
- Students should be reminded to set aside personal differences and act professionally when working with peers.

- A variety of theoretical models should be taught in a way that students can decide for themselves which ones best suit their style of practice.
- When students are engaged in practicums it is up to the instructor to let them know exactly what is expected of them as well as seeing to it that supervisors are fully qualified and fulfilling their roles properly. Instructors should not also be practicum supervisors and must not take money providing student workers.

It is important for instructors to be aware of and abide by the diversification rules mandated by their employer.

<u>Ethical responsibilities of teachers to students</u>

Instructors and supervisors (from henceforth called simply "instructors") who teach in the field of social work have several ethical responsibilities to the students and trainees (from henceforth called simply "students"). First, the instructors should learn the students' limits and the problems they have which might interfere with their education. If a student consistently performs poorly despite warning and added help then it is the ethical duty of the instructor to remove them from the course. Next, if the instructor wishes to hold a class which includes asking the students to reveal information of a personal nature it is made clear to the students that any information they choose to reveal will not be used against them in any way. If a student asks for counseling the instructor should refer them to an appropriate professional and not attempt to counsel the student themselves. Also, individuals who will be seen or treated by students should have full knowledge of the student's standing as defined by the instructor. Last, instructors should emphasis the importance of following a code of ethics.

Research

Social workers must follow a specific code of ethics when engaging in research. Whenever research involves the use of human subjects all local, state and federal laws regarding their treatment must be followed. It is also important that the research be culturally applicable to the people involved. If at any time the research strays from standard practice the researcher must ask other professionals for their viewpoint and document everything carefully. Researchers must be sure that the subjects are in no way harmed during the course of the study and should interfere with their daily lives as little as possible. Even when a social worker is participating in a larger research project they are solely responsible for their actions and maintain ethical practices.

Performance of ethical research

Ethical standards are in place to guide social work research. First, the social worker should not lie to the participants unless it is absolutely fundamental to the research then the lie should be reveled and explained as soon as possible. Second, all participation should be on a voluntary basis. Third, just as in regular counseling sessions all that the social worker learns during research is confidential. Fourth, if participants are minors or others who cannot give their informed consent then informed consent must be obtained from their guardians. Fifth, once data has been collected the researcher should answer any questions the participant may have. Last, when two or more social workers collaborate on research they must keep any agreements made to one another.

Ethical reporting of research results

The following is an explanation of ethical issues surrounding the reporting of research results. Social workers must tell of any factors which may have skewed the results. Next it is important to present data as accurately as possible and to interpret data only as is indicated by the study. Social workers must never falsify results or use misleading interpretations. Even if the research does not lead to the data expected by the study the social worker has a responsibility to release the information and try to explain why the outcome may have occurred. Unless given permission by research participants all data must be anonymous as to the participants' identity. Whenever asked by other professionals appropriate information must be provided for research replication.

Ethical research publication

It is important that all laws involving copyright are followed when publishing research results. All participants involved in performing a research study should be given proper credit according to generally accepted practice. The leader of the study should be listed first; unless someone else (including a student) contributed the majority of the information, in the list of authors. Any photos, tables, or graphs included in the publication should be properly credited. If a paper has been given to a publisher for review then it can not be given to another publisher until the first has made a decision. All articles and papers should undergo a peer review process. Social workers who are asked to be a part of a peer review board must accurately report their findings and must not accept any money for their participation. Also they may not disclose any proprietary information.

Ethical violations

Unfortunately ethical violations do sometimes occur in the field of social work. When violations do happen the social worker has an ethical responsibility to the profession to act in a certain way.

- The social worker should remain familiar with the current code of ethics and review them as necessary.
- If the social worker is not sure ethical rules are being broken they should ask for help from another social worker to decide.
- If the violations are happening at the employer level then the social worker should talk to the direct supervisor pointing out the violations and the corresponding ethical code.
- When the social worker believes that another social worker is behaving ethically she should first talk to the colleague about the problem.
- If after speaking to the misbehaving colleague they do not change or correct the behavior then the social worker must report the ethical breach to the proper authorities.

Social workers must never accuse an individual of unethical behavior without sufficient cause.

Client rights

Clients have certain rights afforded to them on the basis of ethical therapy. A counselor must always explain to the client on a level which they can easily understand all modes of therapy, assessment tests and results, possible risks or benefits, and goals. Clients should also fully understand how payment is to be made and the number of sessions most likely required. Any method of supervision, the client's right to refuse treatment and the right to access treatment records should be known to them.

Clients must also be able to make choices for themselves about therapy issues. These issues may include who to receive therapy from and the types of assessments used except in those cases were it does not benefit the client. If the individual client is unable to give their consent either because they are under age or due to lower mentally faculties then the above rights should be explained to the client's guardian.

Some practices that are ethically wrong for the social worker to do

In some cases a social worker should refuse treatment, refer the client to another professional, or limit their access to a client. If for example, the social worker is currently treating Bill Smith she should not without permission of Mr. Smith and great thought on her own part enter into a therapeutic relationship with Bill's wife. In this scenario it would be best to refer Mrs. Smith to another social worker.

A social worker must never engage in sexual congress with a current client. This rule extends a full two years after the therapist-patient relationship is over. If after two years a social worker wishes to have an intimate relationship with a former client then they must record that the relationship will not harm the former client and is in no way manipulative on the part of the social worker. Social workers should not treat individual's with which they already have a non-counseling relationship. This includes family and friends. Co-workers whether of a higher or lower rank should also not be taken on as clients.

Self supervision and continuing education

Self supervision should be consistent and ongoing. Self supervision includes being sure that personal feelings are not coming into play within the therapeutic relationship, that skills are up to date and that the client makeup is a mirror of the community in which the social worker practices. Over time a social worker may feel that he is not performing to the level that his qualifications suggest he should be. Because the field of social work is not static it is important to obtain continuing education. Social workers may want to keep their previously learned skills sharp, learn how to practice new types of therapy or learn to work with new types of people. Continuing education should be an ongoing process for the ethical social worker.

Outside supervision

After a social worker has been practicing for some time they may begin to feel out of touch with the counseling trends or feel that they are not performing to a high level. This might happen for a number of reasons including, lack of continuing education, new theories and types of therapies, or loss of mental or physical faculties. At that point he should ask a colleague to supervise his work and suggest areas in which he might improve, how to improve, or if improvement is not possible. Another time to ask for the help of a colleague is when ethical decisions must be made and the social worker is unsure of the best outcome. If for example the social worker is counseling a couple who wish to have private sessions as well, he may ask for advice, without releasing confidential information as to the appropriateness of private sessions.

Sexual harassment

An area of public responsibility deals with sexual harassment. Sexual harassment has a two part definition. The following behaviors are the first part of the definition for sexual harassment: asking for sex, trying to hug or kiss another person, talking about sex or making sexual innuendos, and making sexual gestures. The second part of the definition of sexual harassment states that the above behaviors make the job place a difficult place to work, are unwanted and are morally offensive. This part of the definition is based on what the average person would find reasonable (not sexual harassment) or unreasonable (sexual harassment). For example, if Mark Smith and Jane Jones work in the same office and Jane says, "Mark, you look nice today." this would not be considered sexual harassment. However, if Jane said, "Mark you look totally sexy in those tight jeans. Why don't you come closer so I can get a better look?" this may be considered sexual harassment.

Supervision and Professional Development

Supervision areas

There are three main areas of social work supervision: administrative, educational, and supportive. On the company level is administrative supervision. Administrative supervision deals with the practices of the group and responsibility to the outside community. The main focus of the administrative supervisor is to interpret policy and create the day to day jobs done by the social workers in the group. They must also be sure that the job gets completed and is performed properly. Educational supervision also known as clinical supervision works to improve the social worker's counseling skills and help them to become more aware of their own beliefs and problems. Educational supervisors may sit in on counseling sessions, listen to recordings of sessions or read session notes in order to evaluate the social worker's relationship to the client. Supportive supervision focuses on work related stress. The supportive supervisor works to create a good, supportive and stimulating place to counsel.

Purpose

The primary focus of supervision in social work is to increase the individual's counseling aptitude, apprehension and perspective so that they can be more effective counselors for their clients. Proper supervision increases the chances that the client will get better. There are several other reasons that supervision is performed. First, insurance companies will not pay for counseling unless the social worker is formally supervised. Second, in order to receive certification from professional social work agencies the social worker must first have a set number of supervised counseling hours. Third, if a social worker wishes to receive a state license they must have a set number of supervised counseling hours as well. Last, many social work agencies request that their social workers are supervised to maintain the clients' welfare.

Qualifications of supervisor

Social workers who wish to work as supervisors must first undergo a compliment of continuing education classes in order to be properly prepared for the job. Being a supervisor includes working as a teacher and administrator instead of just a counselor. The following qualifications are listed by the National Council on the Practice of Clinical Social Work as necessary for performing as social work supervisor. The social worker must:

- hold a clinical level license
- have worked as a counselor for a minimum of three years
- not have a current ethical case against them
- take a number of courses in supervision and actively work for the continuing improvement of supervision
- have knowledge of the organization's policies and client makeup
- have knowledge of the assets to be found in the local community.

Goals

There are two primary goals in social work supervision case management and personnel development. While both of these goals may be achieved in the same session of supervision it should be remembered that the most important thing in supervision is the job performance of the social worker. During a supervisor session there are number of tools which can be used by both the supervisor and social worker. These tools include case histories, tape-recordings of client sessions, video recordings of client sessions and ideas for acting out certain types of client-counselor situations. When developing the abilities of personnel it is important to have a baseline record of how the individual is performing to begin with. Together the supervisor and social worker should go over the baseline performance readings and plan to increase the social worker's knowledge and skill in areas in which they are week. The code of ethics and the organizations policies should be held into account when making any educational plans.

Documenting supervision

Documentation of supervision sessions are important to prove that the sessions actually took place when agencies ask for a set number of hours of supervision in order to obtain a license or certificate. The supervisor should keep the following in their records:

- date and length of the session
- notes on each session
- a list of things to do next and reasons why
- dates when sessions were cancelled
- dates and notes on all phone and email interaction.

Also within the documentation should be a written agreement specifying the following things about the supervision:
- the nature of the relationship between the supervisor and social worker
- the reason that the supervision is occurring
- what each person is expected to do and what they should expect from the other person
- the supervisors qualifications
- what things will be confidential and what things may be reported
- any necessary financial requirements
- how long the supervision will continue
- how the supervision should come to an end.

Cognitive behavioral based supervision

The cognitive behavioral based supervisor works from the point of view that families hold onto improper behavior because it helps them in some way. The following are typically used to describe the cognitive behavioral supervisor:
- it is the job of the supervisor to educate the counselor in the actions that will best help their clients
- the supervisor must be highly trained
- the expertise needed to be a good social worker can be taught
- the supervisor always keeps the theories of cognitive behavior in mind when planning the supervision process.

There are three types of cognitive behavioral supervisors that pose a problem to the teaching process:
- the very sweet and kind supervisor makes behaviors seem too simplistic
- the overbearing supervisor believes they are never wrong

- the touchy-feely supervisor tells the counselor that how they feel towards a client is more crucial than their beliefs and theoretical foundation.

Models

Integrationist model

A supervisor who uses the integrationist model of social work supervision creates new ideas based on theories already in place. This type of supervisor works by the following criterion:

- the style of supervision is based on the individual counselor being supervised
- the first take of any supervisor relationship is a learning what the counselor needs
- use more than one type of supervision
- ask the counselor what type of supervision they would like and work best with
- work from a structure that is sensible
- change the style of supervision as necessary
- when deciding on the supervisory approach first think about the type of therapy being used
- assess the stage that the counselor is in
- assess the way that the counselor learns best
- think about the counselor's personality
- consider the counselor's aptitude in therapy
- appraise the end results.

Skovholt and Ronnestad model

In their model of social work supervision Skovholt and Ronnestad emphasize the continued growth of the counselor throughout their career. They gave a series of stages for the counselor to follow in order to facilitate growth. The counselor is as such at each of the following stages:

- educated in the theory and practice of social work but not completely trained
- begins to add to their skills from sources outside of their primary education
- try duplicate the practice of others in order to become better
- the start of self-determination
- investigates different styles of practice
- forms a merger of knowledge and style to a single solid belief
- breaks away from the theories and beliefs of others to form their own

- solidifies self conception.

ASiCT

The Adaptive Supervision in Counselor Training (ASiCT) model of social work supervision is based on a four different supervision types. The first type is technical director. The supervisor who acts as a technical director gives the counselor a lot of guidelines about general topics but not very much specific help. Teaching mentor is the second type of ASiCT supervisor. In this role the supervisor gives a lot of guidelines on general counseling skills and also works to bolster the counselor's confidence. The third type of supervisor is the supportive mentor. In this style of supervision the counselor usually takes the initiative in asking for help. The supportive mentor gives the counselor few guidelines but works hard to improve the counselor's self-confidence. Delegating colleague is the final type of ASiCT supervisor. In the role of delegating colleague the supervisor works as a partner with the counselor offering small amounts of guidelines and emotional support.

Practice Evaluation and the Utilization of Research

Case history and naturalistic observation

Case histories allow the evaluator to view the process of counseling from start to finish on a random or non-random sample of clients. They are able to see which methods were used most effectively by the social worker. They can also monitor the rate of recovery for specific problems, see how long the average counseling relationship lasts, get a feel for the social worker's style of counseling and check for ethically appropriate behavior. However reviewing case histories can take a lot of time and are biased towards the social worker as it does not allow for the client's point of view. Evaluation of a particular counseling relationship may also be achieved through the process of naturalistic observation. Evaluators watch the client go about their daily tasks to see how they are functioning. This can be done at set or random time periods during a course of therapy. This method of data collection only allows for the evaluation of one client at a time so is best suited to evaluating a particular social worker and their methods.

Collecting data

Three ways in which data may be collected for research purposes are laboratory observation, surveys and tests. Laboratory observation allows the researcher to place the subject into a specific environment and view their responses to the stimuli. There are two main problems with this type of data collection:
- only a small number of people can generally be studied
- the artificial environment of a laboratory may produce results contrary to what would happen in the natural world.

Surveys and tests are similar methods of data collection as most can be given to a large number of people at once. Surveys ask participants to fill in questionnaires and can be made to measure a wide range of information. The problem with surveys is they may not be representative of an entire population and people may lie on them. Tests take many formats from pencil-and-paper to computerized or object manipulation. Tests must be normed using a representative sample of the community and held under standardized conditions for data collection to be accurate.

Study of development on people

Social workers may wish to study the effects of aging (development) on individuals. Two research methods to study development are cross-sectional and longitudinal. The cross-sectional method looks at different individuals at different stages of development. The researcher compares the findings of one developmental stage to another to look for similarities and differences. The main problem with this method is that because the subjects did not grow up at the same time as one another it is not possible to take in environmental factors as possible reasons for differences. The longitudinal method chooses a group of individuals and follows their development over a set time span. In this research environmental factors are held roughly the same for each individual and so do not have as large an impact on the findings. The problem with this method is that it takes a lot of time to complete.

Scientific method

The scientific method is a way to gain information about the world. For the scientific method to work properly the following things are necessary:

- the data that are collected must be completely true
- the researcher and the research tools must be as disinterested as possible
- information should be tested and retested before it can be considered true
- the researcher must be willing to accept the results even if they are different from what they expected.

The scientific method is used to explain why things happen. In order to do this the researcher must follow specific steps to have a good study. The researcher first formulates a theory, second he makes an hypothesis, third he tests the hypothesis, and last he accepts or rejects the hypothesis on the basis of the research outcome.

Statistics

Data from research are anal sized using statistics. Statistics are able to describe data and are used to decide whether or not the data support, and if they do support then how they support the research hypothesis. The term statistically significant is used when there is a true difference between two sets of data. Statistical significance is based on the laws of probability, the likelihood that outcome "X" will occur given the conditions "A" and "B". For use in social work probability must be less than .05 to be statistically significant.

There are two different types of hypotheses. First, the "null hypothesis" is the idea that two groups have no bearing on or relation to one another. Second, the "alternative hypothesis" is the idea that two groups do have a bearing on or relation to one another. The alternative hypothesis is tested using an experimental and control group.

Problems with statistics

Although statistics are widely used and relied upon in social work science there are several problems with them that should not be overlooked. First, statistical outcomes can be manipulated by the researcher according to which test they use to measure the data. Second, a researcher may "throw-out" data they feel is too far from the mean. When they do this the overall mean will be changed and a different outcome may occur when comparing means. Third, many individuals misunderstand the meaning of statistical significance. If a study finds a statistically significant difference between the null hypothesis and the alternative hypothesis this does not mean that the alternative hypothesis is true. Finally, many people outside of the social work field are unfamiliar with statistics and therefore very likely to not understand the results at all.

T-test

One of the most used statistical tests is the t-test. The t-test is sued to examine whether or not the mean outcome difference of two groups is statistically significant. As with all tests of statistical significance there are three primary things which can change the outcome of the t-test. First, is the mathematical difference between the two means. Usually if the difference is small it will be because of chance rather than experimental factors. Second, is the amount of people or things in the experiment. The lower the number of subjects the more likely the difference is due to chance. This is because unknown factors are not as likely to be cancelled out as they would be in larger groups. Third, is the standard deviation. Standard deviation measures how far apart individual results are. If the standard deviation is small then it is unlikely due to chance.

Scales of measurement used in research

The four scales of measurement are nominal, ordinal, interval and ratio. When using a nominal scale numbers are used to represent different groups. For example using 1 to represent married subjects and 2 to represent unmarried subjects. Ordinal scales also look at different groups but adds the feature that allows us to know which number represents something of a lower degree. For example asking a client to rate how they feel on a scale of 1 to 5. Interval scales add the feature of equal distance between the numbers of measurement. For example using 1, 2, 3, 4 to stand for the grade a school child is in. Ratio scales have all the characteristics of the other scales but also have a starting point of absolute zero. Using pounds or kilograms to measure weight is an example of a ratio scale.

Service Delivery

Community psychology

Community psychology was first developed in the 1970's and has a number of distinguishing factors. First, community psychology places important on how well individuals and communities function. It also recognizes that all people and communities are different and that these differences are healthy and good for all involved. Prevention of mental health problems is the primary goal of community psychology. Generally speaking community psychology does not focus on or work with individuals in a one to one basis but instead focuses on macro level problems and prevention. Community psychology recognizes that research must be done in communities and looked at in order to find out what a particular community needs or how well a program all ready in place is working rather than relying on data taken from other perhaps unrelated sources.

Community psychology viewpoint of mental health problems

Community psychology is based on the ecological perspective which looks at the many environmental factors that influence behavior. A social worker who functions as a community counselor accepts that all people are different and that there is no one right way for people to behave. Instead of focusing on mental health problems from an individual point of view the community social worker looks to the commu8nity and the individual's inability to fit in as the problem. Often rather than requiring the individual t change the community counselor encourages the community to accept the individual as is. Helping the individual to fit in is also achieved by changing the options available in the community.

Community social work

Social workers who wish to work as community counselors must be trained in a number of areas in order to best serve the community in which they work. They are trained:
- how to create programs that will meet the communities needs and desires
- how to find and use the resources already available to the community
- in bringing a community together to work towards a common goal
- to be consultants

- how to co-ordinate and arrange for mental health programs within the community
- how to make sure problems do not start
- to tell whether existing services are working properly
- in how to write grants in order to bring financial resources to the community
- to understand what the community needs in the way of mental health services
- to be a positive voice for the community
- to intervene when problems do occur
- how to bring the programs to the people who need them
- how to train others to work with the community
- to understand what happens to bordering systems when one system changes.

Community service delivery

Three common models of community service delivery are the clinical/community, community/clinical, community-activist and academic/research. First, the clinical/community model. Social workers coming from this point place a higher importance on individual psychological health than other types of community counselors. They usually work in community health centers or hospitals. Second, the community/clinical model places the majority of its focus on the community at large and usually works to create new programs for use by the entire community. The community-activist social worker typically works to be a positive voice of the community, oppose civil inequality and determines were money is being misused and was to use that money instead. The final model for service delivery in communities is the academic/research model. As the name implies social workers who use this model spend most of their time performing research, deciding how the results can best be used by the community and teaching others to implement programs.

Service models

Some service models of community psychology are prevention, social-ecology, evaluation/policy-analysis, and consultation. The prevention model lets social workers create new services for the community based on the number of people with mental health problems and how those people are spread out within the community. Viewing community problems based on a social-ecology model requires the social worker to observe the many factors which interact in a community to cause problems for individuals. When social workers rely o data collected from current programs and use it to change those programs or create new ones they are using an evaluation/policy-analysis model. Finally the consolation model is used to educate individuals within the community as well as people outside of the community about the community.

Prevention

Primary prevention

Primary prevention is community based social work which tries to completely wipe out those things which cause mental health problems. It also creates a means to identify individuals that have a tendency for mental health problems and help them before serous effects occur. Primary prevention lowers the total number of mental health illnesses that occur as well as the percentage that they occur within the community. One type of primary prevention is education. An example might be a service that teaches parents the warning signs of depression in children and adolescents and how to communicate more effectively with them. Another type of primary prevention is screenings. Pediatricians may screen parents for stress level for example in an effort to prevent child abuse.

Secondary prevention

Secondary prevention helps to lower the number of people within a community suffering from serious mental disorders. Social workers may spot children during a school screening day that show signs of a mild behavioral disorder. By spotting these children and getting them help as quickly as possible the social worker prevents further more difficult to resolve problems. An organized example of secondary prevention was begun by Emory Cowen and called the Primary Mental Health Project (PMHP). The PMHP looks for children who are having a difficult time in school. These children are singled out for lessons in self-confidence, self-control, and other valuable tools for making school a more comfortable place for them. Secondary prevention may also include specialized mental health emergency rooms.

Tertiary prevention

Tertiary prevention is quite different from primary and secondary prevention. The goal of tertiary prevention is not to lower the number or percentage of people with mental illnesses but to work as an advocate for people with mental health problems and look for ways to support them within the community setting rather than in a mental hospital. Social workers involved in tertiary prevention may live and work in a group home for the moderately mentally retarded. It would be the social worker's job to maintain order and discipline, to lead the house members in group decision making and to be sure that the welfare of all the individuals is looked after.

Justice

Retributive justice

Within the area of community social work it is important to know the various definitions and types of formal and informal justice. One type of justice is known as retributive justice. In this type of justice an individual is punished in a measure equal to their crime. Retributive justice is also known as "an eye for an eye" which is based on Biblical text. An example of retributive justice is the death penalty for a murderer. This system believes that no crime is so minor as to escape punishment, and that jail sentences are more effective than other types of punishment even if they only accomplish keeping the criminal away from society for a prescribed time.

Procedural justice

Important to the functioning of communities is how justice is served. Procedural justice deals with the process of justice rather than the type of punishments given to wrong doers. John Rawls describes three types of procedural justice. Perfect procedural justice involves using a disinterested party to decide what is fair and that the course of action will lead to a legitimate conclusion. Imperfect procedural justice uses a disinterested party but odes not include a method assuring a legitimate conclusion. Pure procedural justice has only a method assuring a legitimate outcome. Furthermore there are three well known models of procedural justice. The participation model which can be helpful in community situations allows the injured party to be an active part of the justice process. The balancing model wishes to find justice but without undo cost. For example, putting a boy on trial for breaking a window would cost far more than the monetary worth of the window and so would not be an acceptable practice under the balancing model. The outcomes model focuses everything on the end result. As long as the result is just then it is unimportant how the results were reached.

Strict egalitarianism

Strict egalitarianism is the process of distributive justice in which everyone is given an equal share of resources. This principle works on the idea that all people are equal. The main problems with this model are indexing and timing. Indexing refers to the method of how the resources will be dispersed. One way to disperse resources is to give everyone an equal amount of everything. For example, if there are five people in the group and there are 10 bananas, 5 pieces of bacon, and 20 hours of hair dressing services to be distributed then each member will receive 2 bananas, 1 piece of bacon and 4 hours with the barber. On the surface this appears to be a good solution however one of the member may be a bald vegetarian so that member would suffer while the others gained. Time is another problem because if each individual starts with the same amount of something over a period of time the number each person has will become unequal.

Principles

Difference principle

The difference principle of distributive justice requires that individuals who produce the most resources get the most resources in return (usually in the form of money). This method acts as a catalyst encouraging people to work harder in order to receive a larger portion of the community's wealth. The problem with this type of distribution is that people do not have equal access to jobs that allow for high production or are at a disadvantage within the system due to inadequate education or healthcare. For this model to work properly all individuals must start from an equal footing and there must be no bias in hiring practices. This model also leads to some people having much less than others which in itself may be seen as a form of injustice.

Resource based principle

The resource based principle (sometimes called resource egalitarianism) of distributive justice gives community members an equal amount of resources to begin with and then does not interfere with the end results. This model maintains that each individual should be treated the same and without bias by the community. However, individuals who are born with medical, mental or intelligence problems receive more resources than other individuals to help make up for the handicap. The resource based principle also tries to make up for deficiencies in natural talents (as opposed to talents that are learned and developed over the lifespan). This attempt to measure talent is the biggest flaw in this model because talents can be subtle or difficult to categorize.

Welfare based principle

The welfare based principle of distributive justice highlights the well-being of the individual. Goods and services are given to people according to what will give the most good to the largest number of people. For example if a group is made up of ten people and there is $10,000 to be dispersed between them it would necessarily be correct to give each of them $1,000. Instead the percentage of money given to each person in the group would be worked out according to the benefit of each person. Deciding how to measure "benefit" is the main problem of this theory. Also the welfare based principle can end up being very unfair to some people.

Desert based principle

The desert based principle of distributive justice looks at what each person deserves as the way to disperse resources within the community. There are three main models for desert based distribution: contribution, effort and compensation. According to the contribution model individuals are given resources based on the usefulness of what they give to the community. For example a doctor that saves lives would receive more resources than a street sweeper. According to the effort model individuals are given resources based on the amount of energy and exertion they put into the job they do. For example a street sweeper who works hard ten hours a day would receive more resources than a doctor who only worked one hour a day. According to the contribution model individuals are given resources based on the damage (financial, physical or mental) they receive while on the job. For example a coal minor who risks his life would receive more resources than a gardener.

Libertarian principle

In the libertarian principle of distributive justice the focus is on the way that resources are dispersed rather than the amount of resources any one individual receives. This model is often used when dealing with property rights rather than goods or services. An individual that obtains property must do so in a fair manner and must leave enough property for others to use. For example if a community member purchases the city park, paying for it a reasonable fee, they must still allow other members of the community to use the park land or make other park lands available to the community in order for the purchase to be completely fair.

Administration

Management

Communication and interpersonal relationships

There are a number of important tasks for social work administrators within the realm of communication and interpersonal relationships.

- Able to speak and write effectively in order to reach their goals.
- Resolves problems in an informal and easy manner arriving at solutions which are agreeable to all parties involved.
- Good at reading people and their relationships.
- Able to get meetings done on time while accomplishing what they set out to do.
- Described as a team player.
- Able to begin and maintain cooperative groups.

As advocates social work administrators should be educated in how policy change can be effectively accomplished at the organizational, community, state and national levels. Also they should stand firm in their beliefs and actively work towards the betterment of their clients.

Administrator duties

Finances

Social work administrators must often take up the task of dealing with the practices of financial dealings. In order to do this job well they must have a good background and education in the following:

- how to propose new deals, accept new deals, write contracts and accept contracts
- how to find, request and gain financial resources from a variety of areas including private corporations and endowments and public charities and trusts
- how to handle the group's money in an honest, transparent and capable manner
- how to write, implement and educate staff on the need and use of budgets
- how to read financial reports and write them in an easy to understand manner being sure they are kept on file and/or distributed to the appropriate people.

Leadership and governance

Social workers who work as administrators must be good leaders and govern fairly. Good leaders learn the strengths of their colleagues and use them to best help the entire team. Also they instill the strong desire to work hard and well in their followers. Good leaders are able to deal with all manner of problems a high level of skill. Coming to a decision and standing by it is another aspect of leadership. Leaders bring people together to work on common goals without creating problems. Good leaders care also risk takers when the ends justify the means.

Social work administrators must also govern efficiently and effectively. In order to do this they must clearly understand the rules of the group in which they work. Also they should have general knowledge about the many ways that organizations can be structured. Outside of their own association they must be able to work with organizations which oversee social work practice.

Human resource management

Some social workers may fill the roll of human resource manager in their workplace. In this case it is helpful for the social worker to have a background in human resources or to complete courses in continuing education on the subject. Part of the job that a human resource manager does is to hire new staff, train new staff or current staff to fill particular roles, to encourage and facilitate staff development and be sure that the individual and the job they perform are a good fit. It is important for human resource managers to stay abreast of the current personnel policies within their organization as well as in the field of social work generally. Finally a human resource manager must maintain a working knowledge of all laws surrounding hiring practices in their area.

Program development and organizational management

Social work administrators often fulfill the important tasks of program development and organizational management. Program development refers to the creation of new forms of service delivery to clients within the workplace as well as creating services to maintain staff education, morale and safety. Such programs may include parenting classes for clients or a course on sexual harassment in the workplace for employees. Organizational management requires the social work administrator to know the theory of management that their organization uses to maintain order as well as a general knowledge of organizational management within the framework of social work practice. A wide comprehension of health and human services is also necessary in order to develop good programs and organize well.

Human Resource Management

Although typically associated corporations, human resource training and development practices can be used by social workers in a community setting in order to train volunteers, organize committees or develop future leaders. Social workers use three stages during the development and implementations of instruction sessions. First, they decide what type of training is necessary. This may be done by taking a survey of the community members, reviewing town hall meeting transcripts, or consulting with other professionals who serve the community. Next, a training program is created. Often times community members have a strong desire to help out but do not have the necessary skills needed.

Training programs

Training programs work best when the students have strong motivation, are allowed to practice new skills as they are taught, and receive high levels of response from the teacher. For the best outcome the instructions sessions should mirror the actual "job" requirements as closely as possible. Once instruction has begun and again after completion it is important to be sure that the individuals are learning the appropriate skills and putting those newly learned skills into appropriate practice. This may be accomplished by giving the students a chance to model behavior during the training sessions, on sight inspections once the students have been placed or by using comment cards filled out by the community members who use the service.

On-the-job training

Volunteers can be an important part of community intervention practices. Often people who wish to volunteer have a high level of personal motivation but a low level of necessary skills. There are several ways that volunteers can be trained in a community setting. The most common type of corporate training (corporate training is a good model for community training in many aspects) is "on-the-job training". This method of training is inexpensive; generally people who have been volunteering for some time train the new volunteers. It is also fast as volunteers can begin to help out immediately. On-the-job training is also highly effective since the skills are learned while being used they become more firmly entrenched in the volunteer.

Simulation training

While often used for highly technical jobs, simulation training can be used in a community setting for training human resource volunteers. Simulation training is accomplished by using a "mock-up" of the actual job sight and situation. This type of training can be used for educating community member in what to do in case of a natural disaster or other highly stressful crises situation. The community social worker in conjunction with police, hospitals, firefighters, etc may plan a day long recreation of a crises event. First, the community workers will advise the participants in what will happen during the training. These instructions should be as close to what would be done in the event of an actual crisis. The simulation is then carried out. Afterward, the participants should be debriefed as to what worked and what could be improved upon.

Community resource training

Community members may be quite effectively trained in a classroom setting. Because resources such as time, money and facilities are often at a premium in community work in-class training is normally used for brief instructions, such as three hours, only. For example, a community social worker may conduct a class on emergency intervention techniques one Saturday afternoon a month. This type of training is most effective students are given a chance to practice the skills learned. In some cases programmed instruction may be used in the place of classroom instruction. Programmed instruction is a course of self-paced study using workbooks, online instruction, or a combination of both. This type of instruction is best used with highly motivated individuals who do not have the time to devote to in-class training. Examples of programmed instruction are: grant writing, volunteer organization formation, and leadership skills.

Incentive motivation

When working in a community environment it is important for the social worker to understand the reasons people are motivated to perform particular behaviors. Incentive motivation is defined as "an attracting force". That is when individuals work because of incentive motivation they want to gain or receive something through their actions. People work harder when they expect a large reward than they do if the reward is small.

When using a reward system with clients, social workers should be aware of a few basic facts.

- The sooner the reward is given after the desired behavior the stronger the bond between behavior and reward will become.
- It may take larger and larger rewards to get the client to behave in the desired fashion unless the behavior in itself is rewarding in that it improves the client's quality of life.

Individuals work harder for rewards if a reward is not given every time the behavior is performed once the behavior-reward connection has been established.

Sample Test Questions

1) In treating a client in crisis, the caseworker should focus on

(a) the immediate presenting problem

(b) a few specific problems in day-to-day functioning

(c) a wide range of problems in day-to-day functioning

(d) underlying personality problems

2) A social worker is interviewing a new patient who presents some symptoms of depression. The patient reports recent changes such as diminished functioning, marked weight gain, early morning awakening, fatigue, inability to concentrate, suicidal thoughts and headaches. The patient mentions that he started a new medication for a medical condition three weeks ago. The worker would first:

(a) arrange a psychiatric consultation in order to have an anti-depressant prescribed

(b) ascertain the prescribed medication and investigate its side-effects

(c) proceed with a thorough psychosocial history and precipitating events

(d) hospitalize this patient until the suicidal ideation passes

3) A social worker is utilizing environmental manipulation as a technique when he/she:

(a) represents the agency at a health and welfare council meeting

(b) uses a psychosocial framework

(c) suggests the use of psychoactive medications

(d) helps the client find more satisfying employment in a supportive environment

4) A diagnosis of Schizophreniform Disorder is generally applied to clients whose psychotic symptoms:

(a) are related to substance abuse

(b) are very long term

(c) show a marked and continuing decline in functioning

(d) are similar to those of schizophrenia and have existed more than one month, but less than six months.

5) A 15 year old female patient at a mental health clinic complains that for the past three weeks she has been uncharacteristically angry and irritable and has had difficulty concentrating on school work. She says that she feels "down in the dumps". Her appetite has diminished and though weighing 120 pounds a month earlier, she has lost 9 pounds. She has difficulty sleeping and has withdrawn from after school activities that she had previously found interesting and enjoyable. During the interview she seems constantly in motion, rising several times and walking around the room before returning to her chair. It is most likely that she is suffering from:

(a) a drug induced depression

(b) a somatoform disorder

(c) a depressive episode

(d) an adolescent behavior disorder

6) The policy of providing Permanency Planning refers to:

(a) children who are at risk of removal or are removed from their own homes

(b) the development of a plan through which abused and neglected children will be assured of a stable family situation throughout childhood

(c) a stable foster care plan for children removed from their homes

(d) the use of adoption for children at risk

7) DSM-IV-TR permits certain diagnoses for mental disorders to be made, even though the diagnosis does not totally fit DSM-IV-TR criterion. These diagnoses are normally modified by the word:

(a) revised

(b) provisional

(c) temporary

(d) latent

8) A social worker and his agency supervisor are sued for malpractice by the family of a teen age boy who made several attempts at suicide and finally succeeded in killing himself. Which statement best reflects the supervisor's legal status in this lawsuit?

(a) Since the supervisor was not the direct clinician and had never personally treated the youth, she is not liable for any negligent actions committed by others in the agency.

(b) The supervisor shares vicarious legal liability and is responsible for carefully monitoring and evaluating the status of every case under treatment by her supervisees, and for keeping records concerning the supervisee's work on the case.

(c) The agency is the only legally liable party and the workers are not individually responsible.

(d) In cases such as these, parents often believe that a finding of negligence on the part of the clinician will reduce their sense of loss and failure. The lawsuit is probably frivolous and neither the worker, nor the supervisor is responsible.

9) A patient presents at an ambulatory care facility and is in obvious psychological distress, showing severe anxiety and paranoia. The clinician is unable to determine the exact configuration of the patient's symptoms, but is certain that it is an Anxiety Disorder. The worker is unable to determine if the is order is primary, caused by the patient's severe kidney disease or related to other factors such as the patient's continuing substance abuse. The most likely DSM-IV-TR diagnosis is;

(a) Anxiety Disorder, with generalized anxiety

(b) Anxiety Disorder, undifferentiated

(c) Anxiety Disorder, NOS

(d) Anxiety Disorder, provisional

10) A school social worker interviews a 15 year old male student with an IQ of 70. Though assigned to slower classes, the student maintains social relationships and is able to respond appropriately to teachers and class mates. His school work is within the range that would be expected for his recorded IQ. He can read (somewhat below grade level) and is able to do very basic arithmetic. He is also able to follow instructions and is generally amiable in responding to coaching and correction. In developing a plan with this student and the family, the social worker would:

(a) plan for eventual supervised residence in a facility for the mentally disabled

(b) establish a plan that includes vocational preparation and that will eventually lead to independent living.

(c) emphasize vocational achievement in the near term

(d) provide coaching and tutoring to improve his reading

11) A DSM-IV-TR diagnosis of a specific disorder generally includes a criterion of:

(a) a clinically significant impairment, or distress in a social, occupational, or other important area.

(b) a description that includes an identifiable etiology

(c) distress that exceeds 6 weeks

(d) no medical involvement

12) A DSM-IV-TR diagnosis:
(a) provides sufficient information for developing a treatment plan
(b) ends the treatment planning process
(c) is insufficient by itself for treatment planning
(d) is an early or intermediate step in the treatment planning process.

13) A DSM-IV-TR diagnosis often includes a specifier or suffix to delineate the severity of the disorder. The usual specifier is:
(a) mild, moderate or severe,
(b) in partial remission
(c) in full remission
(d) prior history

14) A client begins treatment with a social worker and tells the social worker that he must promise never to involuntarily hospitalize him no matter how depressed or suicidal he may seem. The underlying ethical principle that determines the social worker's response is:
(a) The obligation to start where the client is
(b) The expectation that the client has good reasons to raise this issue.
(c) The need to do what is necessary to keep a severely ill client from ending treatment.
(d) Never to make a promise that is in conflict with legal and ethical requirements.

15) A social worker who attempts to impose her judgments on clients is most likely to elicit clients':
(a) acquiescence
(b) cooperation
(c) resistance
(d) appreciation

16) In a first interview, a worker observes that the client moves slowly, with stooped posture, talks slowly and in a lifeless way, lacks spontaneity, and shows little change in facial expression as they discuss the client's problem.
The worker would most likely suspect:

(a) depression

(b) a manic stage

(c) anxiety

(d) delusional thinking

17) In a first session at an HMO mental health clinic with a couple who want to address marital problems, the wife complains that the biggest problem in their marriage is the husband's nasty temper. The worker's best response is:

(a) can you tell me more about this problem?

(b) 2.have you done anything that might provoke his anger?

(c) at our session today he doesn't seem to have a problem with self control.

(d) to ask the husband if he wishes to discuss his problems with his temper

18) A social worker at a health center is working with a young adolescent group concerned with drug and alcohol prevention. The social worker is uneasy about conflicts within the group and is fearful that they may interfere with group process. The worker's supervisor might initially:

(a) seek to delineate and resolve the worker's personal history with regard to conflict

(b) communicate support, indicating that controversy and conflict may be normal and natural means for resolving issues

(c) inquire about the concerns of the worker and reflect back the issues without resolving them

(d) suggest that the worker not reach any conclusions and bring in any issues which might arise

19) Children who suffer physical, mental or emotional injuries inflicted by caretaking adults are commonly termed:

(a) children of poverty

(b) abused or neglected children

(c) developmentally masochistic

(d) victims

20) Under most state laws, mental health professionals must alert child welfare agencies or other lawful authorities to:

(a) suspicion of child abuse

(b) evidence of child sexual abuse

(c) imminent threats to a child

(d) child custody battles

21) **A supervisor wants to observe a supervisee's client interview through a two way mirror. Because the supervisor is a professional staff member with overall responsibility for all cases in treatment by staff, the worker would:**

(a) not need to obtain the client's informed consent since the observation's purpose is supervision

(b) not have to obtain informed consent of the client, since such consent is given when clients sign a release form for information at intake

(c) have to obtain the client's informed consent on the observation and its use

(d) have to obtain informed consent only if the session is to be recorded

22) **A social worker is conducting a small counseling group. The members seem to have some difficulty in beginning. A statement the worker would not make is:**

(a) In what way can I help you to begin?

(b) Who might like to begin?

(c) It's sometimes difficult to begin

(d) It seems hard to begin today

23) **A hospital patient is referred to social services after she complains of insufficient money for food. After talking with the patient, the worker's diagnosis is that the patient, although from a low income family, is not indigent. She seems to consistently have difficulties managing money and does not appear to handle her funds appropriately. Her diet appears nutritionally adequate. The worker's most suitable action would be to:**

(a) help the patient obtain assistance from a casework agency for help with money management

(b) provide continuing casework treatment through the hospital social service department to insure that her diet remains adequate

(c) suggest to the patient that she apply to the public welfare agency to determine eligibility for public assistance

(d) reassure the patient that her income can be made to cover her essential needs

24) **A social worker using a psychosocial casework approach is not likely to:**

(a) consider the client-worker relationship to be a basic therapeutic tool

(b) rely on psychiatric diagnostic-classifications

(c) be concerned with the client's interaction with the environment

(d) frequently use novel, unconventional treatments

25) The process of assessment is the task of the:

(a) social worker

(b) client

(c) social worker and the client

(d) agency psychiatrist

Answer Key

The correct answer is (a): The immediate presenting problem as it is perceived by the client is the only possible arena in which a social worker can intervene. Other responses will be perceived by the client as non-responsive to his or her concerns.

The correct answer is (b): Medications can have powerful side effects and should be ruled out as a causative factor. 1. a psychiatric consultation is unnecessary at this time 2. the clients current mental state and inability to concentrate suggest that a psychosocial history will not be feasible.

The correct answer is (d): Environmental manipulation suggests the employment of specific changes in the client's life that will improve their immediate situation.

The correct answer is (d).

The correct answer is (c): The only other possible answer is 1, however drug use is not mentioned as a factor in the girl's life and no history of drug use is cited.

The correct answer is (b): It is the most general answer and describes the broad outlines of the policy's intention in regard to children at risk.

The correct answer is (b): This is a fact question and is unambiguous.

The correct answer is (b): A supervisor is legally responsible for cases under supervision and shares personal responsibility with the supervisee. The agency is also liable since their agents performed the actions leading to the alleged damage.

The correct answer is (c): This is a fact question. NOS is an abbreviation for Not Otherwise Specified.

The correct answer is (b): The youth's functioning seems appropriate for his IQ and his achievement are within normal range. The question refers to the development of a plan and the answer should reflect a planning response. Given the youth's age and high functioning, it is likely that he can eventually find employment and live independently. This should be a focus of the social worker.

The correct answer is (a): This is a fact question and refers to specific criteria of DSM-IV-TR.

The correct answer is (d): 1 is incorrect since DSM-IV-TR is descriptive. 2. Is incorrect as treatment planning is dynamic and continues throughout treatment. 3. does not account for the need for narrative that captures the tone and attitude of family members. A DSM-IV-TR diagnosis is ordinarily an early step in the diagnostic phase of work with the client and is normally an early stage of treatment planning.

The correct answer is (a): This is a fact question and is based on information found in DSM-IV-TR.

The correct answer is (d): Answer 1 refers to a practice principle not an ethical principle. Answer 2 is irrelevant and 3 would seem opportunistic and manipulative. The social worker's obligation is to be honest and make his or her professional obligations clear to the client.

The correct answer is (c): Resistance usually occurs when a practitioner attempts to impose a judgment that a client is not prepared to accept.

The correct answer is (a).
 No other response fits the constellation of factors described in the question.

The correct answer is (a).
It is the only response that is responsive to the wife's statement.

The correct answer is (b).
In this question, the correct response is the one that emphasizes the supervisor's educational function, while reassuring the worker that conflict is a part of group process. Answer 1. - helping the worker deal with his or her own issues regarding conflict alters the supervisory relationship and tilts it into a therapeutic situation.
Answers 3 and 4 do not help the worker with the immediate problem.

The correct answer is (b).

The stem of the question is a common definition of child abuse.

The correct answer is (a).

A good faith child abuse report requires only that the worker suspect that abuse has occurred. Evidence (response #2) is a much higher standard and is not required for a report.

The correct answer is (c).

When third parties are viewing sessions it is ethically imperative that the client is aware of the situation. Even if they have previously signed a release, the worker is required to let the client know when actual observations are taking place.

The correct answer is (a).

The other three responses place the responsibility on the group to find a way to begin interacting. Answer number one places the responsibility on the worker and suggests that it is the worker's obligation to take charge. The worker's role is to encourage and reflect to the group.

The correct answer is (a).

After identifying money management as the primary problem, the best strategy is to provide help for the problem. The other three responses are not germane to the client's presenting problem. She neither needs public assistance or assistance with nutrition issues since she has an adequate diet.

The correct answer is (d).

All of the issues described in responses 1-3 are part of the psychosocial approach. Novel or untested approaches would not be used without the permission of the client.

The correct answer is (c).

Assessment is a shared responsibility of client and social worker. It is also a pragmatic approach to achieving client cooperation in working on the identified problems.

Secret Key #1 - Time is Your Greatest Enemy

Pace Yourself

Wear a watch. At the beginning of the test, check the time (or start a chronometer on your watch to count the minutes), and check the time after every few questions to make sure you are "on schedule."

If you are forced to speed up, do it efficiently. Usually one or more answer choices can be eliminated without too much difficulty. Above all, don't panic. Don't speed up and just begin guessing at random choices. By pacing yourself, and continually monitoring your progress against your watch, you will always know exactly how far ahead or behind you are with your available time. If you find that you are one minute behind on the test, don't skip one question without spending any time on it, just to catch back up. Take 15 fewer seconds on the next four questions, and after four questions you'll have caught back up. Once you catch back up, you can continue working each problem at your normal pace.

Furthermore, don't dwell on the problems that you were rushed on. If a problem was taking up too much time and you made a hurried guess, it must be difficult. The difficult questions are the ones you are most likely to miss anyway, so it isn't a big loss. It is better to end with more time than you need than to run out of time.

Lastly, sometimes it is beneficial to slow down if you are constantly getting ahead of time. You are always more likely to catch a careless mistake by working more slowly than quickly, and among very high-scoring test takers (those who are likely to have lots of time left over), careless errors affect the score more than mastery of material.

Secret Key #2 - Guessing is not Guesswork

You probably know that guessing is a good idea - unlike other standardized tests, there is no penalty for getting a wrong answer. Even if you have no idea about a question, you still have a 20-25% chance of getting it right.

Most test takers do not understand the impact that proper guessing can have on their score. Unless you score extremely high, guessing will significantly contribute to your final score.

Monkeys Take the Test

What most test takers don't realize is that to insure that 20-25% chance, you have to guess randomly. If you put 20 monkeys in a room to take this test, assuming they answered once per question and behaved themselves, on average they would get 20-25% of the questions correct. Put 20 test takers in the room, and the average will be much lower among guessed questions. Why?

1. The test writers intentionally writes deceptive answer choices that "look" right. A test taker has no idea about a question, so picks the "best looking" answer, which is often wrong. The monkey has no idea what looks good and what doesn't, so will consistently be lucky about 20-25% of the time.

2. Test takers will eliminate answer choices from the guessing pool based on a hunch or intuition. Simple but correct answers often get excluded, leaving a 0% chance of being correct. The monkey has no clue, and often gets lucky with the best choice.

This is why the process of elimination endorsed by most test courses is flawed and detrimental to your performance- test takers don't guess, they make an ignorant stab in the dark that is usually worse than random.

$5 Challenge

Let me introduce one of the most valuable ideas of this course- the $5 challenge:

You only mark your "best guess" if you are willing to bet $5 on it.
You only eliminate choices from guessing if you are willing to bet $5 on it.

Why $5? Five dollars is an amount of money that is small yet not insignificant, and can really add up fast (20 questions could cost you $100). Likewise, each answer choice on one question of the test will have a small impact on your overall score, but it can really add up to a lot of points in the end.

The process of elimination IS valuable. The following shows your chance of guessing it right:

If you eliminate wrong answer choices until only this many answer choices remain:	1	2	3
Chance of getting it correct:	100%	50%	33%

However, if you accidentally eliminate the right answer or go on a hunch for an incorrect answer, your chances drop dramatically: to 0%. By guessing among all the answer choices, you are GUARANTEED to have a shot at the right answer.

That's why the $5 test is so valuable- if you give up the advantage and safety of a pure guess, it had better be worth the risk.

What we still haven't covered is how to be sure that whatever guess you make is truly random. Here's the easiest way:

Always pick the first answer choice among those remaining.

Such a technique means that you have decided, **before you see a single test question**, exactly how you are going to guess- and since the order of choices tells you nothing about which one is correct, this guessing technique is perfectly random.

This section is not meant to scare you away from making educated guesses or eliminating choices- you just need to define when a choice is worth eliminating. The $5 test, along with a pre-defined random guessing strategy, is the best way to make sure you reap all of the benefits of guessing.

Secret Key #3 - Practice Smarter, Not Harder

Many test takers delay the test preparation process because they dread the awful amounts of practice time they think necessary to succeed on the test. We have refined an effective method that will take you only a fraction of the time.

There are a number of "obstacles" in your way to succeed. Among these are answering questions, finishing in time, and mastering test-taking strategies. All must be executed on the day of the test at peak performance, or your score will suffer. The test is a mental marathon that has a large impact on your future.

Just like a marathon runner, it is important to work your way up to the full challenge. So first you just worry about questions, and then time, and finally strategy:

Success Strategy

1. Find a good source for practice tests.
2. If you are willing to make a larger time investment, consider using more than one study guide- often the different approaches of multiple authors will help you "get" difficult concepts.
3. Take a practice test with no time constraints, with all study helps "open book." Take your time with questions and focus on applying strategies.
4. Take a practice test with time constraints, with all guides "open book."
5. Take a final practice test with no open material and time limits

If you have time to take more practice tests, just repeat step 5. By gradually exposing yourself to the full rigors of the test environment, you will condition your mind to the stress of test day and maximize your success.

Secret Key #4 - Prepare, Don't Procrastinate

Let me state an obvious fact: if you take the test three times, you will get three different scores. This is due to the way you feel on test day, the level of preparedness you have, and, despite the test writers' claims to the contrary, some tests WILL be easier for you than others.

Since your future depends so much on your score, you should maximize your chances of success. In order to maximize the likelihood of success, you've got to prepare in advance. This means taking practice tests and spending time learning the information and test taking strategies you will need to succeed.

Never take the test as a "practice" test, expecting that you can just take it again if you need to. Feel free to take sample tests on your own, but when you go to take the official test, be prepared, be focused, and do your best the first time!

Secret Key #5 - Test Yourself

Everyone knows that time is money. There is no need to spend too much of your time or too little of your time preparing for the test. You should only spend as much of your precious time preparing as is necessary for you to get the score you need.

Once you have taken a practice test under real conditions of time constraints, then you will know if you are ready for the test or not.

If you have scored extremely high the first time that you take the practice test, then there is not much point in spending countless hours studying. You are already there.

Benchmark your abilities by retaking practice tests and seeing how much you have improved. Once you score high enough to guarantee success, then you are ready.

If you have scored well below where you need, then knuckle down and begin studying in earnest. Check your improvement regularly through the use of practice tests under real conditions. Above all, don't worry, panic, or give up. The key is perseverance!

Then, when you go to take the test, remain confident and remember how well you did on the practice tests. If you can score high enough on a practice test, then you can do the same on the real thing.

General Strategies

The most important thing you can do is to ignore your fears and jump into the test immediately- do not be overwhelmed by any strange-sounding terms. You have to jump into the test like jumping into a pool- all at once is the easiest way.

Make Predictions

As you read and understand the question, try to guess what the answer will be. Remember that several of the answer choices are wrong, and once you begin reading them, your mind will immediately become cluttered with answer choices designed to throw you off. Your mind is typically the most focused immediately after you have read the question and digested its contents. If you can, try to predict what the correct answer will be. You may be surprised at what you can predict.

Quickly scan the choices and see if your prediction is in the listed answer choices. If it is, then you can be quite confident that you have the right answer. It still won't hurt to check the other answer choices, but most of the time, you've got it!

Answer the Question

It may seem obvious to only pick answer choices that answer the question, but the test writers can create some excellent answer choices that are wrong. Don't pick an answer just because it sounds right, or you believe it to be true. It MUST answer the question. Once you've made your selection, always go back and check it against the question and make sure that you didn't misread the question, and the answer choice does answer the question posed.

Benchmark

After you read the first answer choice, decide if you think it sounds correct or not. If it doesn't, move on to the next answer choice. If it does, mentally mark that answer choice. This doesn't mean that you've definitely selected it as your answer choice, it just means that it's the best you've seen thus far. Go ahead and read the next choice. If the next choice is worse than the one you've already selected, keep going to the next answer choice. If the next choice is better than the choice you've already selected, mentally mark the new answer choice as your best guess.

The first answer choice that you select becomes your standard. Every other answer choice must be benchmarked against that standard. That choice is correct until proven otherwise by another answer choice beating it out. Once you've decided that no other answer choice seems as good, do one final check to ensure that your answer choice answers the question posed.

Valid Information

Don't discount any of the information provided in the question. Every piece of information may be necessary to determine the correct answer. None of the information in the question is there to throw you off (while the answer choices will certainly have information to throw you off). If two seemingly unrelated topics are discussed, don't ignore either. You can be confident there is a relationship, or it wouldn't be included in the question, and you are probably going to have to determine what is that relationship to find the answer.

Avoid "Fact Traps"

Don't get distracted by a choice that is factually true. Your search is for the answer that answers the question. Stay focused and don't fall for an answer that is true but incorrect. Always go back to the question and make sure you're choosing an answer that actually answers the question and is not just a true statement. An answer can be factually correct, but it MUST answer the question asked. Additionally, two answers can both be seemingly correct, so be sure to read all of the answer choices, and make sure that you get the one that BEST answers the question.

Milk the Question

Some of the questions may throw you completely off. They might deal with a subject you have not been exposed to, or one that you haven't reviewed in years. While your lack of knowledge about the subject will be a hindrance, the question itself can give you many clues that will help you find the correct answer. Read the question carefully and look for clues. Watch particularly for adjectives and nouns describing difficult terms or words that you don't recognize. Regardless of if you completely understand a word or not, replacing it with a synonym either provided or one you more familiar with may help you to understand what the questions are asking. Rather than wracking your mind about specific detailed information concerning a difficult term or word, try to use mental substitutes that are easier to understand.

The Trap of Familiarity

Don't just choose a word because you recognize it. On difficult questions, you may not recognize a number of words in the answer choices. The test writers don't put "make-believe" words on the test; so don't think that just because you only recognize all the words in one answer choice means that answer choice must be correct. If you only recognize words in one answer choice, then focus on that one. Is it correct? Try your best to determine if it is correct. If it is, that is great, but if it doesn't, eliminate it. Each word and answer choice you eliminate increases your chances of getting the question correct, even if you then have to guess among the unfamiliar choices.

Eliminate Answers

Eliminate choices as soon as you realize they are wrong. But be careful! Make sure you consider all of the possible answer choices. Just because one appears right, doesn't mean that the next one won't be even better! The test writers will usually put more than one good answer choice for every question, so read all of them. Don't worry if you are stuck between two that seem right. By getting down to just two remaining possible choices, your odds are now 50/50. Rather than wasting too much time, play the odds. You are guessing, but guessing wisely, because you've been able to knock out some of the answer choices that you know are wrong. If you are eliminating choices and realize that the last answer choice you are left with is also obviously wrong, don't panic. Start over and consider each choice again. There may easily be something that you missed the first time and will realize on the second pass.

Tough Questions

If you are stumped on a problem or it appears too hard or too difficult, don't waste time. Move on! Remember though, if you can quickly check for obviously incorrect answer choices, your chances of guessing correctly are greatly improved. Before you completely give up, at least try to knock out a couple of possible answers. Eliminate what you can and then guess at the remaining answer choices before moving on.

Brainstorm

If you get stuck on a difficult question, spend a few seconds quickly brainstorming. Run through the complete list of possible answer choices. Look at each choice and ask yourself,

"Could this answer the question satisfactorily?" Go through each answer choice and consider it independently of the other. By systematically going through all possibilities, you may find something that you would otherwise overlook. Remember that when you get stuck, it's important to try to keep moving.

Read Carefully

Understand the problem. Read the question and answer choices carefully. Don't miss the question because you misread the terms. You have plenty of time to read each question thoroughly and make sure you understand what is being asked. Yet a happy medium must be attained, so don't waste too much time. You must read carefully, but efficiently.

Face Value

When in doubt, use common sense. Always accept the situation in the problem at face value. Don't read too much into it. These problems will not require you to make huge leaps of logic. The test writers aren't trying to throw you off with a cheap trick. If you have to go beyond creativity and make a leap of logic in order to have an answer choice answer the question, then you should look at the other answer choices. Don't overcomplicate the problem by creating theoretical relationships or explanations that will warp time or space. These are normal problems rooted in reality. It's just that the applicable relationship or explanation may not be readily apparent and you have to figure things out. Use your common sense to interpret anything that isn't clear.

Prefixes

If you're having trouble with a word in the question or answer choices, try dissecting it. Take advantage of every clue that the word might include. Prefixes and suffixes can be a huge help. Usually they allow you to determine a basic meaning. Pre- means before, post- means after, pro - is positive, de- is negative. From these prefixes and suffixes, you can get an idea of the general meaning of the word and try to put it into context. Beware though of any traps. Just because con is the opposite of pro, doesn't necessarily mean congress is the opposite of progress!

Hedge Phrases

Watch out for critical "hedge" phrases, such as likely, may, can, will often, sometimes, often, almost, mostly, usually, generally, rarely, sometimes. Question writers insert these hedge phrases to cover every possibility. Often an answer choice will be wrong simply because it leaves no room for exception. Avoid answer choices that have definitive words like "exactly," and "always".

Switchback Words

Stay alert for "switchbacks". These are the words and phrases frequently used to alert you to shifts in thought. The most common switchback word is "but". Others include although, however, nevertheless, on the other hand, even though, while, in spite of, despite, regardless of.

New Information

Correct answer choices will rarely have completely new information included. Answer choices typically are straightforward reflections of the material asked about and will directly relate to the question. If a new piece of information is included in an answer choice that doesn't even seem to relate to the topic being asked about, then that answer choice is likely incorrect. All of the information needed to answer the question is usually provided for you, and so you should not have to make guesses that are unsupported or choose answer choices that require unknown information that cannot be reasoned on its own.

Time Management

On technical questions, don't get lost on the technical terms. Don't spend too much time on any one question. If you don't know what a term means, then since you don't have a dictionary, odds are you aren't going to get much further. You should immediately recognize terms as whether or not you know them. If you don't, work with the other clues that you have, the other answer choices and terms provided, but don't waste too much time trying to figure out a difficult term.

Contextual Clues

Look for contextual clues. An answer can be right but not correct. The contextual clues will help you find the answer that is most right and is correct. Understand the context in which a phrase or statement is made. This will help you make important distinctions.

Don't Panic

Panicking will not answer any questions for you. Therefore, it isn't helpful. When you first see the question, if your mind goes blank, take a deep breath. Force yourself to mechanically go through the steps of solving the problem and using the strategies you've learned.

Pace Yourself

Don't get clock fever. It's easy to be overwhelmed when you're looking at a page full of questions, your mind is full of random thoughts and feeling confused, and the clock is ticking down faster than you would like. Calm down and maintain the pace that you have set for yourself. As long as you are on track by monitoring your pace, you are guaranteed to have enough time for yourself. When you get to the last few minutes of the test, it may seem like you won't have enough time left, but if you only have as many questions as you should have left at that point, then you're right on track!

Answer Selection

The best way to pick an answer choice is to eliminate all of those that are wrong, until only one is left and confirm that is the correct answer. Sometimes though, an answer choice may immediately look right. Be careful! Take a second to make sure that the other choices are not equally obvious. Don't make a hasty mistake. There are only two times that you should stop before checking other answers. First is when you are positive that the answer choice you have selected is correct. Second is when time is almost out and you have to make a quick guess!

Check Your Work

Since you will probably not know every term listed and the answer to every question, it is important that you get credit for the ones that you do know. Don't miss any questions through careless mistakes. If at all possible, try to take a second to look back over your answer selection and make sure you've selected the correct answer choice and haven't made a costly careless mistake (such as marking an answer choice that you didn't mean to mark). This quick double check should more than pay for itself in caught mistakes for the time it costs.

Beware of Directly Quoted Answers

Sometimes an answer choice will repeat word for word a portion of the question or reference section. However, beware of such exact duplication – it may be a trap! More than likely, the correct choice will paraphrase or summarize a point, rather than being exactly the same wording.

Slang

Scientific sounding answers are better than slang ones. An answer choice that begins "To compare the outcomes..." is much more likely to be correct than one that begins "Because some people insisted..."

Extreme Statements

Avoid wild answers that throw out highly controversial ideas that are proclaimed as established fact. An answer choice that states the "process should be used in certain situations, if..." is much more likely to be correct than one that states the "process should be discontinued completely." The first is a calm rational statement and doesn't even make a definitive, uncompromising stance, using a hedge word "if" to provide wiggle room, whereas the second choice is a radical idea and far more extreme.

Answer Choice Families

When you have two or more answer choices that are direct opposites or parallels, one of them is usually the correct answer. For instance, if one answer choice states "x increases" and another answer choice states "x decreases" or "y increases," then those two or three answer choices are very similar in construction and fall into the same family of answer choices. A family of answer choices is when two or three answer choices are very similar in construction, and yet often have a directly opposite meaning. Usually the correct answer choice will be in that family of answer choices. The "odd man out" or answer choice that doesn't seem to fit the parallel construction of the other answer choices is more likely to be incorrect.